*To Amy
From a very
Roman Susel
June 6, 2022*

In Search of Snow

Roman Susel

Copyright @ 2018 Roman Susel
All rights reserved
ISBN - 10 1775258807
ISBN - 13 978-1-7752588-0-3

DEDICATION

To my cherished nine grandchildren, encouraging
them to persevere in following their dreams
and to savor the joys of creation.

In Search of Snow

Snowflakes are very fragile creations, yet so powerful when united.

DISCLAIMER

This is a work of fiction. Names, characters, places, and incidents are products of the author's imagination and are used fictitiously. The characters involved are wholly imaginary and their opinions should not be confused with the author's.
Any resemblance to actual events, locales or persons, living or dead, is entirely coincidental.

CONTENTS

	Introduction	1
1.	Snow and Roaring Wind	3
2.	Enjoying the Snow	32
3.	The Festive Season	67
4.	Good Fortune	109

ACKNOWLEDGEMENTS

I thank the all knowing for blessing me with a loving family, a restless curiosity and with manageable aches and pains, enabling me to pursue my dreams. I am very grateful for the encouragement, inspiration, love and guidance given to me by my loving and very supportive wife, Wanda and our four sons, Roman J, Tim, Chris and Ted, their significant others and our nine grandchildren. Thank you for believing that I could record my recollections with ardor.

Introduction

My adventure began on the geologically oldest of the main Hawaiian Islands, the island of Kauai also known as the "Garden Isle". Kauai is the fourth largest of these islands and the 21st largest island in the United States. Kauai's weather is pleasantly warm year-round. Even in the coolest month of January, daytime highs average 78 F (26 C) and the evening lows dip to 65 F (18 C). August is the warmest month with daytime highs averaging 85 F (29 C) and cooling off to 75 F (24 C) in the nighttime. The island is home to sharp jagged cliffs, lush green valleys, tropical rainforests and cascading waterfalls. I had met some people from Canada visiting and taking photos of the 151-foot-tall, 40-foot-wide Opaekaa Falls near the Wailua River on Kauai's East Side, the most populated district on the island, which is referred to as the Royal Coconut Coast for the groves of coconut palms that grow there. The Coconut Coast is just north of the city of Lihue, the commercial and government center of the island.

The Canadians and I spoke about snow that they escaped back home by coming to Kauai. In Hawaii snow falls almost every winter on the summits of the three tallest volcanoes; the 13,800-foot Mauna Kea, the 13,600-foot Mauna Loa (the Earth's largest volcano) both on the Big Island, and Haleakala on Maui. Fog, ice, clouds and high humidity plague the summits. Frost and ice is often mistaken for snow especially when seen from a distance. Frost is moisture from humid air that settles on the ground or on plants and freezes into ice. Snow on the other hand forms in the clouds as the ice crystals grow around condensation and then fall to the ground. Frost and snow are dangerous forming black ice on roads making access difficult. The National Weather Service in Honolulu issues winter weather advisories for the summits when conditions merit them. We have had up to eight inches of snow at Mauna Loa and Mauna Kea but varying temperatures see it melt within a few days.

The Canadian visitors talk about snow staying on the ground prompted me to wonder about how people were able to cope and what did it all look and feel like. I did some research and compared temperatures and was amazed by the average snowfall statistics.

Temperatures

Kauai	November	December	January
Day High	81 F (27 C)	79 F (26 C)	78 F (26 C)
Night Low	71 F (22 C)	68 F (20 C)	65 F (18 C)
Quebec			
Day High	41 F (5 C)	28 F (-2 C)	21 F (-6 C)
Night Low	28 F (-2 C)	14 F (-10 C)	5 F (-15 C)

Quebec Snowfall Averages

	November	December	January
centimetres	22	48	52
inches	8 1/2	19	20

Rarely having seen snow, I was intrigued and against the best advice from some friends, I visited Quebec, the land of snow in winter. I toured some of the back roads of the Province of Quebec in Canada. I met many very friendly and welcoming French Canadians and felt very much at home (chez nous) with them. I even started to learn several words in their wonderful French Canadian language. I had the pleasure to meet an elderly man named Felix Anctil Laflèche that everyone called GrandPere Anctil (Grandfather Anctil). During my conversation with him, he sat in a rocking chair with his back to the crackling fireplace, smoking his pipe. We spoke about life in his village. He did most of the talking and I most of the listening. It was a very warm, cozy and tranquil experience.

He was a very interesting individual who bravely spoke English to me and I found the way he spoke fascinating and I took notes. Much later I transcribed my notes and to capture the melodic manner of his speech I wrote his words in rhyming dialect verse and entitled it "In Search of Snow". As presented here the words accompany my paintings of the lovely village scenes in winter. I thank GrandPere Anctil for his recollections which added so much happiness to my visit and wish him and his wife a healthy and happy life ahead. Au Revoir!

1. Snow and Roaring Wind

En visite you come worst time of the year,
Much snow and roaring wind as you now hear.
Frigid cold outside with very strong breeze.
Sit down, stay inside because outside you'll freeze.
The story of my village I tell you while the wind blows
Get closer, near the fire and warm up your toes.

The wind she blow and blow all night long,
Howling loudly her wailing coyote song.
She blow so hard she ring the church bell,
People think its Jean Lamotte come from hell.
Then she swirl and blow chimney smoke,
On rue Principal the hotel window she broke.

At the start were built two fairly large mills,
By the men in the community using their skills.
One mill to saw wood the other to grind grain into flour,
Small dams were built to harness water power.
So we have lumber for houses and flour for bread,
This helped to grow the village and be widespread.

Our early homes were all made of wood,
With good planks we built the neighbourhood.
We also made furniture, barrels, wagons and guns,
And farmed the land with our daughters and sons.
The flour mill is now stand silent there,
Waiting for someone with some savoir faire.

Originally for both mills water was used,
But in winter it froze and people were not amused.
But we learn from railway how to make steam,
So we adapt the mills to run year round supreme.
The saw mill still produce specialty wood cuts,
And on occasion for renovation wooden struts.

Rolland set up a tannery not far from the mills,
But further away from the town toward the hills.
This helped blow the strong odours away from downtown,
He produce leather from elk and deer the best around.
First he cured the skins in lots of salt,
Take out the water and make the bacteria halt.

Then he wash the skins and treat them with lime,
The hides were cleaned and scrubbed of the grime.
He scrape off the hair and soak skins in a tannin bath,
The hides were then dried and continued on their path.
The leather was dressed and finished to make it strong,
It became soft, flexible, waterproof for lifelong.

The snow drifts the wind makes big and high,
By daylight snow like fog cover the sky.
It's so cold and with blinding blowing snow,
The road ahead is unclear, we don't know
Could hit something, maybe a tree.
Have only one excuse that we could not see.

In my early years church was the center of the universe,
And covered everything from cradle to hearse.
It was our school, and philosopher for now and things to come,
And our counselor and advisor for things to overcome.
It was the source of all knowledge, experience and inspiration,
We were a spiritual unit and it merited the loyalty of our generation.

Sixty days after Easter La Fête de Dieux was celebrated by street parade,
With church banners, choirs and white robed altar boys marching in a crusade.
Children clad in black and red cassocks walk and hymns they sing,
People slow marching with candles praying and taking in everything.
Other religious members and nuns their rosaries were reciting,
People lined the street route, decorated their homes and were inviting.

A dozen altar boys before a dais on wheels with gold cloth roof,
With priest and vicars carried the blessed sacrament under a canopy, carried aloof.
The procession distributed graces and blessings to all on the route,
They passed the decorated balconies and windows which were there to salute.
The parish choir and communicants wearing veils and armbands,
All of them holding in prayer their uplifted arms and hands.

In the center of the course an altar was built with many steps or stairs,
On which a service was conducted with singing and prayers.
On the steps were flowers and children dressed as angels were placed,
We celebrated the presence of Christ in the sacrament on which it is based.
The procession moved through the whole village with grace,
Reviving the faith of the faithful and atoning for sins to erase.

Now we no longer have the procession in the street,
The holuiday is still celebrated but is now more discrete.
In big cities we still have St Jean Baptiste parade quite a site,
Each year on June 24 with floats, marching bands and a bonfire at night.
In the big cities the parade is recorded and shown on TV,
So it is available for everyone in the village to see.

In my day we listen to radio CKAC first French station in Amérique du nord,
Started in 1922 and all the people listened and adored.
In 1950 with the help of the church they start "Le Chapelet en Famille",
Cardinal Leger recite the rosary and for the devout it have a great appeal.
For twenty years the program contribute,
For the Marie Reine du Monde Cathedral a tribute.

The rosary is used to count the Hail Mary prayers,

It's a simple model to meditate and praising God for us to declare.
Je vous salue Marie, pleine de grâces, le Seigneur est avec Vous.
Vous êtes bénie entre toutes les femmes et Jésus, le fruit de Vos entrailles, est béni.
Sainte Marie, Mère de Dieu, priez pour nous, pauvres pécheurs,
maintenant et à l'heure de notre mort. Ainsi soit-il.

Hail Mary, full of grace, the Lord is with thee,
blessed art thou among women, and Jesus the fruit of your womb is blessed.
Holy Mary, Mother of God, pray for us sinners,
now and at the hour of our death. Amen.
With the entire congregation reciting these words you know you are blessed,
Filled with peace you know that your worries have been well addressed.

Last year big Willi Blain hit a moose,
In hospital he tell the priest he hit a goose.
Our village is pas grande, in fact it is small,
One terrible catastrophe affects us all.
The wind she blow hard again today,
This time she blow the snow the other way.

They report giant drifts around the bay,
The ice is thick, Yvon he drive his sleigh.
He crossed the river to the other side,
Then come back, no place to hide.
Yvon he call to his Marie, Mon amour,
Come with me chéri, we go on a tour.

She answered shouting in the breeze,
Non Yvon, it's too cold we will freeze.
Yvon say, "Marie, you are right, love is great,
Let's get together and keep warm, the tour can wait.
The wind she blow now weeks on end,
Temperature and snow continue to descend.

Sabastien he buy leather from the tannery a big stack,
He and his wife Simone make a variety of horse tack.
Saddles, stirrups. bridles, halters, bits, harness and reins,
They do fine work even ship some out by the trains.
Each item have big science, they tell you, they know,
Solid equipment make rider and horse a happy duo.

They both very proud of their handiwork and materiel,
Sabastien stand there we say, "Il se pèter les bretelles".
Meaning he fart off his suspenders, bursting with pride,
While Simone simply smile taking it all in stride.
Their work win them a prestigious award worldwide,
For the superb horse tack that they supplied.

We have a potter who work with clay that is gray,
He use his potter's wheel and his hands to shape the clay.
He makes dishes and cups, puts them in the sun to dry,
Makes a variety of beautiful objects for people to buy.
I say do what you can, "fais ce que tu peux,
If you can't do as you want, "si tu ne peut faire ce que tu veux".

The white blanket covers landmarks, farms, houses and the rue,
And every house keeps warm by putting more wood on the feu.
We are very peaceful and remote, but not backward habitant,
Today we have telephone, TV and internet not by accident.
It's true we only have one canal of the TV,
That we use the rabbit ear antenna to get free.

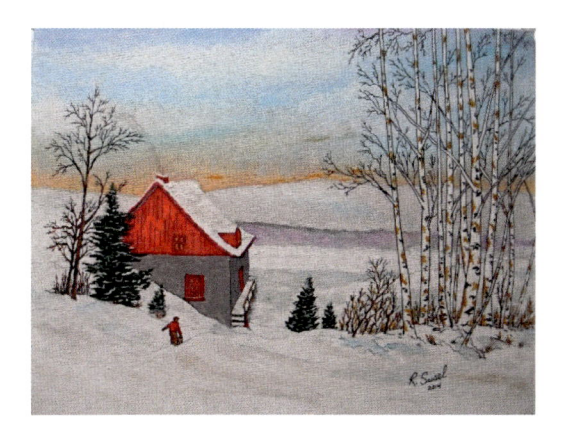

With pay satellite TV we have a lot more to see,
And with radio we get to listen to the big city.
Rue Principal she go to the big chemin highway,
Where Josephine plan to open her brand new café.
Sylvio is the proprietor of the dépanneur,
Everyone shops there even the Monseigneur.

Josephine she work there, make the sandwich,
Coffee and egg salad that is taste good but very rich.
Sylvio also has the only gasoline pump around,
In the village he also had the first truck to be found.
He gets stock delivrez from far worldwide,
Sometime even fresh fruit from outside.

Delivrez trucks souvent stop there,
Sylvio is always busy with little time to spare.
He also sell beer by the bottle or case,
His store is big, we call it a marketplace.
Margaret, Sylvio's wife she help him sometime,
She often think that Sylvio and Josephine commit a crime.

Josephine is one big big flirt,
She keep Margaret and Sylvio on alert.
Sylvio may be looking for some dessert,
Especially when it's in a young skirt.
Margaret is no maudite fool,
She is also a teacher at the school.

School has changed a lot from little house to big place,
We had a pot bellied stove in the middle not a fireplace.
We studied reading, writing, math and catechism,
And got punished by the teacher's terrorism.
We learned how to use a pen nib with real ink,
They teach us behaviour, morality and how to think.

Margaret serves as a midwife too,
She loves little children, very much beaucoup.
Marcel is also work for Sylvio but upside,
When not delivering beer and stuff he sit by the fireside.
He looks after the horse and carriage or sleigh,
He keep secret whatever Sylvio and Josephine do or say.

Inside Sylvio's store was a feast for the eyes and nose,
You are treated to a variety of shapes, colours and rows.
On shelves are foodstuffs, sugar and in the air the aroma of spices,
Pots, pans and patent medicines to take in times of crisis.
Sylvio was a clearing house for local rags, wool and produce,
Dried tobacco, juices, sliced meats, venison and moose.

Josephine she sing soprano in church on Sunday,
She is part of choir as the people pray.
She is big flirt, make big eyes at every man,
People talk and women think she is a boogeyman.
They say she even makes out with the priest,
That part is covered by the confessional rules at least.

At all the sexy gossip Josephine she laugh,
And tells people to prove it with a polygraph.
Her sister Angelique sing in the choir too,
She say Josephine like attention and nothing is new.
Angelique is younger, good head, beautiful and nice,
Make many guys in church dream of paradise.

Her mother Yvette she make tourtiere and is good cook,
Very honest and raised her girls by the good book.
Her father Armand make whisky in the barn,
Damn good stuff Sylvio refused to sell, did no harm.
Armand have more customers than the dépanneur store,
Men come from all over just to explore,

Often the police would come, they could not ignore.
But Armand smart guy hide his stock under the floor,
Until one day he get the Curée drunk,
Who make complaint showing police the whisky in the trunk.
They take Armand away and locked him up for a week,
Armand speak to them about whisky and the mystique.

They enjoy him and let him out, say make a mistake,
Often for them Armand have extra he make.
The Curée was sorry, Yvette make no tourtiere for him,
That make life for the Curée very miserable and grim.
Armand stay away from church now for some time,
Even refuse to give the Curée for the church one thin dime.

He even tell everybody the Curée makes the sacramental wine,
Meanwhile Armand works on his whisky overtime.
Olivier he play the church organ very well,
At Sunday service, weddings and the final farewell.
He also plays the piano at the bar at the hotel,

10

Every Friday night people come to the hotel as clientele.

They drink, tell stories, hear gossip and the nouvelle,
They dance, listen to music, relax and raise hell.
The Curée could collect more money here if he pass the hat,
But although not a sin, that is not so diplomat.
But when the wind she blow so strong and hard,
The doors to the hotel remain tightly barred,

Bastien, the owner, boarded up the broken window,
Cursed the wind for shutting down his bistro.
The wind she blow real hard just now,
Even the pussycat is afraid to meow.
Bastien he sell Armand's whisky, nothing new,
But he call it his special and name it Caribou.

A special blend he say, so nobody knows,
That it comes from Armand's creative studios.
Even the Curée on him a favour he bestows,
He visits, buys some and hide it under his clothes.
He tells Bastien to tell Armand he is sorry he spoke,
And begs his forgiveness to treat their tiff as a joke.

Armand hears that and spits his tobacco in the spittoon,
Saying, "What does the Curée take me for? a buffoon?
Although Armand not go to church because of the Curée,
He strong catholique secure in his faith in every way.
Often and Christmas and Easter he go to neighbouring town mass,
He know more people there and he say it give him some class.

He also bring a quantity of big jugs of booze with him,
I think he make deliveries on the way and then he sings a hymn.
It is so cold that drying clothes outside, they freeze,
They are solid and no longer flutter in the breeze.
Long johns, what have you and even chemise,
Become stiff and that happen across the diocese.

One day Annette, the wife of Laurent bring in the clothes,
The long johns they stand up straight near the stove.
In the window Laurent looked in and see them stand there,
Just back from hunting he aim his gun he shoot and also swear.
He broke his window and shoot out the trap door of his underwear.
He apologize to Annette thinking she had an affair.

Next door to Laurent and Annette lived a young girl Maxine.
She no longer young but that is normal and not unforeseen.
She had a dream to be a couturier and got a sewing machine,
That she had seen in a catalogue or some magazine.
Now she makes clothes, does repair, since the age of nineteen,
Won an award for her gown that was worn by the queen.

Maxine the dressmaker is a milliner too,
She make old clothes into something new.
She sell gloves, aprons, shirts, stockings and caps,
Silk, wool, linen and cotton fabric and scraps.
She have needles, thimbles, scissors, ribbons and bows.
And tablecloths, napkins and curtains for windows.

She makes patterns, latest fashion in her shop,
And she use her husband Emil who serves as a prop.
"I am her pin cushion", Emil often complains,
Although stuck with pins many times, smiling he remains.
But he afraid one day snip snip his manhood goodbye,
The ladies in the shop laugh at the jokes he supply.

My village have too many children to name,
Each famile have at least enough for large poker game.
The Curée so happy, he say there is no shame,
It is as God intended, there is no blame.

The wind is blow hard and moves many a cloud,
Not even allowing rue Principal to get snowploughed.

Ambroise is brother in law of the Curée,
He was railway station master inherited from his grand pere Jean André.
Station built by Grand Trunk Railway and still stands today,
Used to have steam locomotives thunder by every day.
Always lots of men, women and children there,
And the trains sending plumes of coal dust in the air.

The station was on the main line into the Atlantic,
Connecting the west to Montreal and then New Brunswick.
In 1923 Canadian National took over from Grand Trunk,
That day grand pere Jean André got really drunk.
He had little hotel he ran by the railway track,
He rent rooms and provide some small snack.

The station have telegraph and telephone, only place,
It have living quarters for his famille and a fireplace.
Jean André smart man learn Morse code operate telegraph machine,
Keep the station warm in winter and always nice and clean.
His wife Madeleine look after the small hotel,
And all his children serve as extra personnel.

Ambroise look after the freight from an early age,
He expedited it, collected revenue and do everything for no wage.
He inherit the job from Jean André because he know so much,
He have good personality and was honest beyond a touch.
To Ambroise a very funny story he tell,
Which Ambroise tell everybody like some nouvelle.

A travelling man and his wife checked into his hotel,
The man went out his thirst to quell.
His wife try to sleep but big train pass by,
Shake the bed so hard, out of the bed she fly.
She try again, another train do same thing, Sacré beurre!
She complain to Jean André but he no believe her.

The wife insist it's true, swear on her honneur in good faith,
She tell him to lie down beside her and to wait.
Jean André make himself comfortable next to the wife,
That's when her husband returned and exclaimed, "Ah , my life!
He politely ask Jean André just what he was doing here,

That's when Jean André got red faced with fear.

He nervous but calmly tell him that he is waiting for a train,
The husband scratch his head and ask his wife to explain.
She did but Jean André don't like anybody to complain,
He changed their room and bring them a bottle of champagne.
Nothing like that happen to Ambroise on his watch,
He remembered one thing after he drink some scotch.

One night the station receive visit by two drunk men,
Who walked upgrade between the railway tracks, when
They come in and one complains about the long stairway he climbed,
The other didn't mind the stairs but he felt it should be redesigned.
Because the iron banister was much too low.
And in winter no doubt it would be covered with snow.

Big change happen to Ambroise in 1978,
When CNR closed its passenger business at the gate.
He sell his small hotel and it was demolished,
And the railway station was almost abolished.
Most of the line now is used mainly for freight,
It is owned by CNR and Via Rail now who regulate.

Morse telegraph now is not needed so Ambroise retire,
And now we exchange stories and both of us smile.
The time has changed my village beaucoup,
Today more people move here, more homes, j'usque bout!

However they use train to make commute,
To big city where their career they execute.

Funny to watch them jump and run for the train,
They push, they shove, they can really entertain.
When they miss the train and look at their watch in shame,
Frequently they have no one but the train to blame.
Always prenez garde whatever you touche,
Remember, comme on fait son lit, on se couche.

Guillaume is a printer, make invitations, bibles and newspaper,
For his big printing press he is the operator.
Jerome is an apprentice learning the trade,
He is very precise and is totally not afraid.
They publish four page newspaper every week,
They have advertising, news and editor speak.

Clémence and Carol have son Pascal by name,
They send him to boarding school and a médecin he became.
He prefer to work in big city hospital, his expertise very good,
His parents think he would be great for the neighbourhood.
But he only come for vacance, now and then,
I don't think he ever will come back permanent again.

Clémence he act as go between for people with pain,
He call Pascal for advice, diagnose and treatment to explain,
Clémence practice medicine with no license,
But he perform this delicately in complete silence.
He deny that, he say he simply do transcription,
And his son Pascal make the prescription.

Where needed the drugs come in the mail,
For urgency the sick person may voyage by rail.
To the nearest big city and its big hospital,
For big trouble they go to Pascal's hospital, only logical.
The voyage depend on the weather and could be diabolical,
Jean Marie cured himself on the train that was comical.

The train rumble and bounce, shake and bump,
Make Jean Marie massage, pump, slump and jump.
In big city he get off the train nice and quick,
He walk and find his lumbago and sciatic no longer sick.
He not go to the hospital, he walk the street,
Looking for a place to stay the night and to eat.

Pretty girl smile at him and they pleasantly talk,
He say she invite him to her place, so they walk.
First they go to restaurant that was on the way,
They eat real well, have wine and Jean Marie he pay.
She say her name is Annabelle, he find that a pretty name,
He say she was beautiful, long legs, a fantastic dame.

She bring him home and introduce him to a big woman at the door,
To spend the night Jean Marie have to pay not to sleep on the floor.
This way he would have a bed and not a chair,
He look around and see many girls also spend time there.
He and Annabelle go to a room, she have the key,
They spend the night Jean Marie say she was la joie de vie.

In the morning the therapy work worked real well,
But Annabelle was gone and Jean Marie was mad like hell.
His pockets were empty, suitcase gone only his train ticket was left,
Jean Marie complain to the big woman about the theft.
He also reported to her that Annabelle was missing,
The big woman say that Jean Marie was just reminiscing.

The big woman looking eye to eye in Jean Marie's face,
Tell him, "Sorry, please leave, there is no Annabelle in the place.
The police she call and Jean Marie start to be scared,
When she was shouting and the woman's hot temper flared.
He run out, red face, mad and say, "Eh Merde",
For this big city treatment Jean Marie was totally unprepared.

He find his way to the train station and sit on a bench,
With no money he could not even buy a drink his thirst to quench.
Jean Marie came home broke but no more sick,
He say there are many ways to get well, it's no trick.
For therapy he recommend an honest mademoiselle,
But hospitals he is afraid of just like hell.

To this day Jean Marie stay single and unattached,
He not try to find an honest mademoiselle not even scratched.
Clémence apologize to Jean Marie for his original advice,
He tell him he tried his best and not to criticize.
Clémence make notes of Pascal's approach and treatments,
So he could advise his own future patients of their commitments.

He got catalogue from dealer of natural medicine and herb,
That help millions of people he find very good, really superb.
He opened naturalist botanical herb shop,
In his front parlour he store quite a large crop.
Sometime now he give his own new professional advice,
Reduce telephone cost to Dr. Pascal and optimise.

His own expertise, research, experience and exercise,
He even sell a choice of arm and leg support device.
Dentistry is another problem we faced for sure,
To make voyage to big city is no good for the poor.
Guy had a very bad toothache nearly drive him nuts,
He drank Armand's gin which make him sick in the guts.

Very drunk, Guy go to see Florent the blacksmith or forgeron,
Ask him to pull out his tooth, his speech was determined and slow.
He was sure that Florent had the pliers to do the job,
And the tooth really hurt his head was a big terrible throb.
Florent refused saying it's not hygienic and is unwise,
Guy take out his gun and look Florent in the eyes.

He tell him, "You pull it or you will not see the sunrise",
Florent act under duress and have to compromise.
In the fire he placed the pliers to be sterilized,
Then he put them in cold water to be neutralized.
Florent grab the tooth, Guy gave such a loud yell,
Tooth came out, Florent and Guy both were happy as hell.

From that time Florent was the dentist until real dentist come here,
But before each such job he must drink lots and lots of beer.
Florent is always busy making horseshoes, hooks and nail,
Tiring hard work he perform without fail.
He repair wagons, machinery, carriages and sleigh,
His anvil he keep busy hammering every day.

Now with decline of horse drawn vehicles today,
He make weathervanes and artwork from iron throw away.
The wind slows down, whistles and howls then starts anew,
Blowing snow and bring freezing cold through and through.
It is not easy in fact it was hard to make money here,
And then if you have it where do you put it losing it you fear.

The house could burn and your money could disappear,
People hide money in jars, in jardin, not far always near.
Until Caisse Populaire opened its banking system at the church,
Armand never go there, I think he hide his money near the old birch.
The Caisse make big promotion, they make your money grow,
Even give you loan but not groceries on credit like Sylvio.

From the garden people dig up their fortunes of cash,
They hurry to the church blessed Caisse with their stash.
Making money does not come easy for the people living here,
They farm, raise cows, cut logs up north, are very sincere.
In winter the young men from the village disappear,
To live in a lumber camp like a mountaineer.

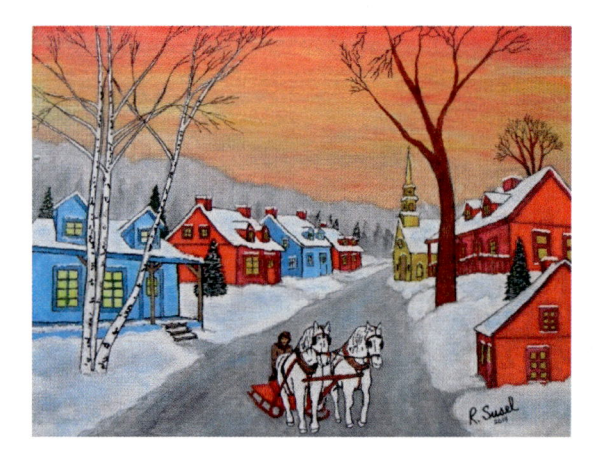

They go up north to cut lumber for big company,
Come home for summer with lots of cash triumphantly.
They see their newborn and start another,
Because new baby need a sister or brother.
Then again they go up north to cut wood,
The mother looks after the home, the father the livelihood.

By tradition the oldest boy was sent to a seminary,
To learn to be a priest or missionary.
Very few go to university or college to make career,
Some join the army because they don't want to farm over here.
They learn a trade, see the world, learn firearm,
The Bon Dieu protect them from any harm.

On the farm there is plenty of work to do,
Feed chickens, milk cows, cut wood, fix this, fix that, adieu.
You know the rich fear death much more than the poor,
The poor work hard and die young, the rich want to endure.
Look at Beauchamp et Freres the funeral people,
They have money higher than the church steeple.

They think a special deal with heaven they enjoy,
And the church cemetery they employ.
Used to be Beauchamp et Fils long time ago,
The father and sons work hard cutting ice you know.
They keep ice for summer in their big shed,
And sell the ice to people for ice box all summer ahead.

They advance from ice to dead people to store,
They put stiffs on ice, ha ha for evermore.
When old man Beauchamp die. people they swore,
Refrigeration and electricity kill him long time before.
Just from the ice business, delivery and stevedore,
He amassed a fortune his sons found under the floor.

Money was not as important when I was young,
We help each other for no pay just cooperation among.
Imagine now they sell fully equipped house to the Eskimo,
Now he pay for electricity, water, gas and radio.
Money now make him crazy, maudite gateaux,

He was happier before in his snow chateau.

Anyway money is here and it is going to stay,
And everybody have to work and then pay.
Giles and Genevieve raise sheep and goats,
He make goat cheese and she sheepskin hats and coats.
With special shears Giles removes the sheep and lamb's wool,
He give Genevieve wool by the basketful.

He so good he start cutting people's hair,
But straight razor shave was a scary affair.
Lots of blood run whenever he try,
Very bad to see the big man cry.
So he use safety razor with replaceable blade,
Say it's more hygienic in the barber trade.

He try new hair style like magazine portrayed,
Sometime good and many time bad I am afraid.
With time he got better and buy a special chair,
He even attempt to cut ladies hair.
But he was chastised and scolded by a lady professor,
And swore that he would never be a hair dresser.

That job was reserved for Monique, wife of Filberte,
She cut, wash, curl, give permanent and hair set.
Women patronize and always go there with no regret,
But Monique she smoke too much cigarette.
Women complain smoke stinks up their clothes,
They prefer the assistant, her sister Rose.

Filberte is quiet he like to repair clocks,
In his spare time he go hunt and trap fox.
He sell the fur to Genevieve in a big box,
As a tip she give him a pair of socks.
She make fur coats and nice warm fur hats,
Make everyone look like aristocrats.

For get together, the community center is in the hotel,
Town meetings, card games and Caisse promotions as well.
Bastien very happy running here and there and he busy too,
Most everybody want to drink a good cold brew.
So busy he hired good looking Marie Claire,
Old Louis sit and carefully watch her he even stare.

He strain his eyes to catch a glimpse of her underwear,
All the while he pretend to play solitaire.
But occasionally he smile at her like he don't care,
She very good looking but that is not my affair.
The Curée outlawed Bingo in the church hall,
Bingo moved to the hotel, anyway the church hall was too small.

Friday night the hotel music was really grande,
The boys got together and formed a band.
Olivier on piano, Luc on guitar, Rene on accordion and Yves on drum,
People dance waltz, jigs and reel until their feet go numb.
Smiling Francois ovation he get for his fiddle he play,

He also sing and dance, turn the place into a real cabaret.

Catch the beat, everybody dance,
Whatever the circumstance, you take a chance.
Ah les fraises et les framboises,
Du bon vin j'en ai bu.
Croyez-moi, chers villageois,
Jamais j'me suis tant plu.

La musique de bons vieux temps, he fiddle away,
And old Sam dance, got carried away and hurt his vertebrae.
People tap their toes all the soiree,
Some got really drunk and fly away.
Bastien happiest of all when he count the cash,
Big smile on his face telling people go home to crash.

Baptiste make very fine wood cabinets,
He supplies for miles around to all the inhabitants.
His wife Giselle help him, have very good eye,
Baptiste's work must be perfect for her to be satisfy.
C'est dommage that for money they are in a tight spot,
Most often to charge for their work they forgot.

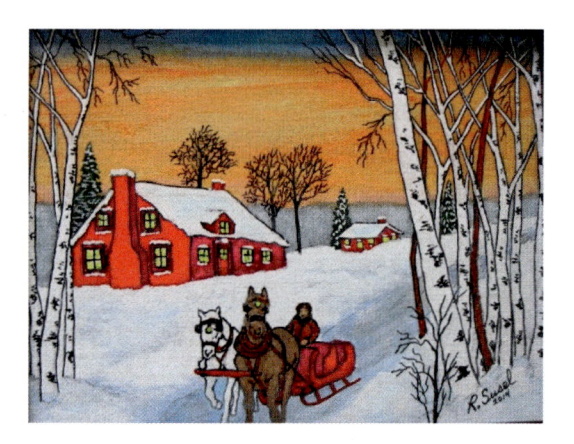

Baptiste produce furniture, bed frames, chairs, rouet and cradles,
He make coffins, shelves, rocking chairs and tables.
He have all sorts of hand tools, a foot powered lathe and saws,
A solid workbench, measuring items to avoid any flaws.
Together with a mortising machine, planes and vices,
Where necessary he even make his own helpful devices.

Furniture factories in big cities give Baptiste competition,
Quality is not as good and the stuff is under suspicion.
They make furniture out of cheap chip wood board,
Made to look nice but after short time need to be restored.
To stay in business Baptiste assemble mass produced parts,
And keep fighting to stay alive unlike his compatriots.

Baptiste the menuisier, he build houses,
Giselle his wife works embroidering blouses.
She weaves yarn threads, makes nice cloth,
Have for sale many napkins and tablecloth.
Every house have a handloom and rouet or spinning wheel,
They spin wool into yarn, make homespun, very ideal.

Like others, she makes quilts, blankets, trousers and coats,
All the while with other singing and trading anecdotes.
The fabric is called "etoffes du pays" and is very strong,
Able to stand lots of ware, it really lasts long.
Baptiste's friend Gaspard se pogne le cul,
Prefers never to get involved not even un peu.

His other friend Fabien likes to chanter la pomme,
Tell big story make him feel like an homme.
Appeler un chat, un chat! are the people I prefer,
Carousers and liars are like a saboteur,
They smile and stab you in the back,
And always claim not to remember, a real amnesiac.

Anselme and Aristide have maple trees and sugar shack,
They tap the trees, work hard almost have a cardiac.
They bottle syrup and even ship some out,
In summer they go fishing mostly catch trout.
Their wives Corinne and Odette weave and knit,
Make beautiful rugs when time permit.

Before we have bakery, each home bake their own bread,
In large brick ovens women made pain de ménage instead.
We ate wonderfully fresh baguettes and pain fesses,
The pungent smell of fresh bread you could not suppress.
Homemade bread like that today you cannot buy,

Just thinking about that give me appetite to retry.

They say in 1617 the first apple tree in the province was planted,
From that French seedling sizeable orchards expanded.
Cider production was in full swing right from the start,
The craftsmanship brought from France came from the heart.
Cider production was outlawed officially until1970 a stranglehold,
It could be produced but legally not able to be sold.

During winter people ate salted pork, deer and caribou,
Ducks and geese were plentiful and partridges too.
Smoked fish and eels from the river were all good to chew,
When the church required that meat not be used on feast days too.
We all liked sour milk, tea cost too much that is true,
A flagon of brandy 'eau de vie" we loved beaucoup.

Gaspard and Manon have big farm for pig,
The place is full of mud, it stinks and not politic.
But the home is clean, Manon is an excellent cook,
Watch her money carefully, good for the pocketbook.
Her pates de cochon, pig's feet are a real treat,
As are the ham and charcuterie, can't be beat.

Antoinette, many lovers have she, people say,
Il n'y a pas de fumée sans feu - and that is okay!
Me I never try because her business is not my affair,
However her ragout de boulettes you cannot compare.
Antoinette at the Caisse Pop she work,
She smile and flirts as a cashier clerk.

Hervé another brother in law of the Curée is the Caisse manager,
He does all the paperwork and is also the janitor.
When men pass the Caisse and the church they tip their chapeaux,
Armand makes face, he laugh and holds tight his dough.
Laissez les bons temps rouler, let the good times roll,
Push some more wood on the fire with the pole.

Antoinette she talks, smiles and flirts a lot,
Be careful, watch out - the stove is hot!
Better to bypass and tip your chapeaux,
In French we say "La poêle est chaud".
Benoit he have a tin shop in town,
He make pails, basins, oil lamps and sells them all around.

He also make eavestroughs and stove pipes galore,
And for his wife Natalie he make a bathtub which she adore.
And he make objects from copper and brass,
Lately he even experiment with fibreglass.
You visit no doubt experience our bécosse,
The outhouse of choice built by Baptiste of course.

The only real bathroom is at the hotel.
They have running water from a tap as well.
Bastien had Baptiste build a water tower for him,
Supplies water to the entire hotel and inn.
They used an old train boiler for the water to heat,
Each room have lots of hot water complete.

Their bathrooms have bathtubs, toilets with nice seats,
On occasion Bastien runs around to fix any leaks.
The toilet sure beats the bécosse outside in the cold,
Have to get in and get out fast otherwise you hold.
Each house for bath use a big basin made of tin,
They fill with hot water from several kettles to begin.

When finished their bath they empty the basin with a pail,
To keep big family clean takes lots of work, travail.
We waited for when sewer pipe will be in place,
The outdoor bécosse not luxury but is no disgrace.
The cold breezy wind she blow in every space,

Alphonse the inventor, want to improve with a fireplace.

People they laugh when they hear his plan,
Baudouin suggested they use a converted old minivan.
That way bécosse is warmer and more portable,
Also he say it is easier to keep more cleanable.
But it cost too much to outfit it from the big city to here,
But it sounded very good to them after a few beer.

We still have the firehouse not far from the mills it appears,
We have a hand pumper fire engine, a ladder truck and volunteers.
The firemen are equipped with axes, hose and pile pole,
If they catch fire early it then is easy to control.
If too late then the orange flames they rapidly spread,
And the volunteers try to rescue people otherwise they are dead.

More stories to tell but we need more firewood,
If the young only knew and the elderly could.
Must tell you about always hungry as a wolf, Onesime,
Skinny as a board but he could eat to an extreme.
He have eye on great cook, large fat Henriette,
She cook for him big assiette of pork and patates.

It was love at first sight, I never forget,
Onesime he eat all day long until the sunset.
The marriage went well and the Curée had them blessed,
The wedding photo was mostly of her very big all dressed.
Onesime stood by thin and somewhat suppressed,
But to give Henriette his love forever he professed.

He loved her and very much her food he sincerely expressed,
All of the guests and Henriette were greatly impressed.
He ate fourteen portions of wedding dinner he confess,
As he kissed her and gave her a loving caress.
They danced and Onesime seemed very stressed,
He was having a hard time holding her and no time to digest.

He fell on the floor. Henriette was very distressed,
They get Clémence to help Onesime get undressed.
Clémence act fast and give him artificial respiration,
No doubt, save his life with no hesitation.
Make him throw up with no regurgitation,
Advise Henriette to look after Onesime with dedication.

He tell her not to feed him too much, maybe he have worms,
Give her some tonic to give him to fight the germs.
Henriette so happy that a widow on her wedding day she would not be,
On her knees she thank God and to look after him she made a plea.
Henriette so happy she start to cry,
Delighted that Onesime did not die.

Watch what you eat Clémence scare her very much,
She also drink tonic and didn't want food to touch.
Henriette cured Onesime from eating a lot,
And she herself much skinnier and smaller she got.
Onesime he complain that half of Henriette he lost,
Half his marriage asset was gone, it had been tossed.

Charlemagne he carve wood, make nice souvenir every day,
His son Coty go to work in Montreal I think for Cirque de Soleil.
He tall, good looking I think he work as a pantomimic,
Now a day's everybody needs some gimmick.
Today my village see beaucoup change,
An antique store, junk yard, doctor, dentist, notaire; it's strange,

Now we don't have to go to big city to do legal affair,
Our village have a new office and an notaire.
He provide legal advice and he go to court,
Handle everything, support, property and transport.
He prepare wills, contracts and deeds,
He knows your rights and where needed he intercedes.

He believe a person is innocent and dumb,
Until that person is proven and bankrupt has become.
In Quebec wills belong to the notaire, public they are not,
So there is no need for probate that would cost a lot.
C'pas des farces that save people time and money,
It's good business and that is not funny.

We have new competition, motel and a medical clinic,
Progress is slow coming but it is not unrealistic.
Myself I'm glad to wake up each morning and see the sunrise,
Each new day has its own problem and surprise.
Its hard sometime to try to verbalize,
Because not everything people do is very wise.

I used to hate weddings because old ladies tell me. "You're next",
They stop that when at funerals I tell them same thing, they were perplexed.
The only time we like to get old is when young we are,
Then life change that and it becomes more bizarre.
People they ask me about getting old, they wag their tongue,
In my opinion the best way to get old is to start young.

I don't worry about age or weight,
Not even about what is on my plate.
I let the doctor worry about that and to fascinate,
That's why I pay them, let them calculate.
Old friend Ambroise changed his testament three times or more,
After keeping secret his new hearing aid he listen to the furore.

Moderne is new and is great, throw out the old,
Then the story of my village would never be told.
If you don't know where you have been,
How do you know where you are going? You just play violin.
That is no criticism of Francois the fiddler I say,
But it is the price that society must pay.

Patrice strong man. he run a wood and coal yard,
He produce split and corded wood and deliver coal, he work hard,
His father before him just saw wood which he sold.
Patrice continue but expand the business fourfold.
He get coal delivered by train and dump in his yard,
Then he take orders and deliver to homes for a charge.

Patrice also start to deliver heating oil,
When it begin to replace coal, and he also sell soil.
He sell and repair oil stove and chimney he sweep,
He work like crazy and he not very cheap.
Have twelve hungry children to feed and wife to keep
He tell everyone that he have no time to sleep.

Anyway the wind continue to blow some more,
But not as strong or hard as before.
Everything moderne not always the best,
Many times it leave you very depressed.
It's not always fits all with one size,
Like I said before not everything people do is very wise.

For instance take hockey, our winter sport,
And Les Canadiens who we all support.
But for youngsters it costs too much,
They must have pads, gloves, head gear and such.
Before we have stick, ice, puck and skate,
Belly full of fire and a skill to appreciate.

On the head we wear a tuque,
And scoring a goal was always a fluke.
Hard to tell what team you're on or who is better,
Because we all wear Les Canadiens sweater.
Now they treat hockey and players like a product,

Build arena, sell tickets, treat it as a market.

Players now get paid lots of money on the ice,
Make promotion, use spreader truck to make ice shiny and nice.
Show youngsters what it takes now to play as if to legitimize,
Parents pay and buy special pads, uniform for big price.
Hockey stick must be composite not wood,
Youngsters must train to have fun if they could.

They dream of having skills to be a superstar,
But not happen to them just look at the histoire.
We play no pads and real wood hockey stick, work up a sweat,
Chase the puck, pass to each other and hit the net.
Norman he skate fast, just see a blurred silhouette,
He knock out his teeth when he go flying over the net.

Why he go so fast when there was no threat,
I really don't know but I never forget.
Old time is better, people have more time to promenade, take a walk,
They gathered more often, visited and had time to talk.
They got along, cooperate, help each other for no pay,
They did not put on airs or ignore as they do today.

I think about that and it give me mal a la tête,
When you see people have so much credit and debt.
This modern notion is very entrenched and widespread,
People should concentrate on being human instead.
They don't think or look very far ahead,
Thank you for listening but now I go to bed.

Bonne nuit Grand Pere Anctil dormez bien, good night,

Many thanks for sharing this history with such appetite.
Sleep well and listen to the howling wind blow,
In the valleys, over the hills and the great plateau.
Blow over your village in the land of ice and snow,
Blanket the houses, the rues, the lakes and the entire tableaux.

2. Enjoying the Snow

Visiting the back roads of the Province of Quebec in Canada, meeting and sharing experiences with many French Canadian inhabitants I felt very much at home (chez nous) with everyone. I was hoping to capture some of the exuberance and decided to record my experience of the visit on paper. I even started to learn several words in the wonderful French Canadian language. I set out to see snow and in the process I not only found it but thanks to GrandPere Anctil I was introduced to many of the local people, given explanations, advice and enjoyed a very warm, loving and cordial stay.

GrandPere Anctil was a very interesting individual who bravely spoke English to me and I found the way he spoke fascinating as I tried to take notes. Much later I transcribed these notes and trying to capture the melodic manner of his speech I wrote his words in rhyming dialect verse, I am truly indebted to and continue to express my sincere gratitude to GrandPere Anctil and his wife Marie-Rose for their companionship, hospitality and cordiality. Merci and Au Revoir!

When GrandPere left, the auberge was deserted and silent,
Even the relaxing cat disappeared and became self reliant.
I decided to take a really fast peek outside just to see
What the potential weather prediction for tomorrow might be.
Millions of snowflakes blowing and dancing all around,
Falling so softly and chasing each other to the ground.

The complete silence was disturbed only by the occasional breeze,
Each gust swirling and pirouetting the snow and rustling the trees.
The penetrating cold was bone chilling as I quietly closed the door.
Very majestic and calming to see but the shivering was hard to ignore.
Back in my warm room I undressed and my pyjamas I quickly put on,
The thick feathery duvet covered bed was inviting me to sleep upon.

So into bed I crept covered up and pulled the duvet up to my chin,
My mind reviewed the stories I had heard and I had to grin.
I thought about snow crystals and how beautifully pictured they are,
How their magnificent structure under the microscope was so bizarre.

The snow fell so silently, so gently and over time became so deep,
The stillness cloaked with fluffy softness lulled me as I drifted off to sleep.

It's morning, and I awoke from my very restful slumber.
I feel refreshed and if anything I suffer from hunger.
My room at the auberge was warm through the night,
Now the sunny brightness in the window added to my delight.
I got up and looking out the window, I could not see outside,
On the outer window a deep crusting of ice had been applied.

This was not a fancy jack frost lacy pattern but sparkly and thick,
Hiding everything from view and very bright, shiny and slick.
Out of bed the room was comfy but somewhat cooled,
I yearn for a hot shower and that is when I was fooled.
The porcelain shower taps were marked with an F and a C,
I wondered Fahrenheit and Centigrade it could not possibly be.

C must stand for Cold so I tried the tap with F instead,
I turned it on full but it got much colder to my dread.
Shivering uncontrollably and growing goose pimples I shut F off,
And curiously turned on tap C expecting a very frigid rebuff.
But oh how welcoming warm water was to my great surprise,
C was steamy, hot, heavenly and brought tears to my eyes.

Then I quickly dressed and descended for breakfast smelling coffee,
I hear familiar noises and see people milling about in the lobby.
People smile, some say bon jour and many other words I hear,
They smile understandably and it sounds like bien dormir.

Don't know who tricked me with the shower taps today,
But I will ask GrandPere he will know what to say.

The oak grandfather clock shows that it is almost eleven,
While my sleepy brain still in a haze thinks that it is only seven.
So here I am having my breakfast called petit dejeuner,
Wondering if GrandPere Anctil was coming in today.
So I sat eating and smiling at everyone, even the cat,
Who skeptically looked at me even surprised at that.

Stamping snow off his boots GrandPere arrived with some fanfare I might add,
Everyone greeted him and he waving and smiling was very glad.
He sat beside me and said Allo mon petit garcon, how are you?
While I luxuriously slept he had been doing his rendezvous.
He was excited and invited me to accompany him in his sleigh,
And said that we would meet many people while we had more café.

I told him that where I come from the shower taps are marked H and C,
H for Hot and C for Cold and in my room they were different how could it be?
He explained that no one tried to fool me; he laughed and said Maudite you got caught!
In French F is Froide meaning Cold and C is Chaud meaning Hot.
Maudite was a new word meaning damn, that I picked up today,
One that I could have used this morning in the shower by the way.

GrandPere said he was up at daybreak yet he looked very rested,
I apologized for sleeping too long but it was okay he protested.
He had already tended to his chickens, pigs, horses and cow,
Even cleared his path and a road or two with his snowplough.
He loved horses and enthusiastically praised and loved them galore,
He said horses were more prepared for winter than we give them credit for.

Horses create their own protection, a naturally warm winter coat,
Beginning to grow their coats as the days are getting short.
Protecting them from cold temperatures, snow and wind all right,
In the cold their hair has suddenly multiplied appearing fluffier overnight.
The hairs lift up and the downy undercoat trap the warm air against their skin,
Preventing heat transfer from them, a clever way to create insulation therein.

In chilling temperatures even the best of coats may not bring enough relief,
Your horse may be uncomfortable and may shiver like you and me in disbelief.
They may need a heavy warm blanket, neck cover or a hood that Sebastien sells,
These must be used carefully to prevent over-heating as Sebastien's wife tells.
If you blanket your horse you'll discover that his hair will lie flat,
If you take the blanket off, his hairs will eventually fluff up to pat.

On a cold day you can warm your hands by pushing them into a horse's coat exact,
The heat you feel there is produced inside the horse's digestive tract.
When a horse slowly digests hay, the fiber ferments and creates heat,
Hay is better than fats and grains because of the fiber the heat does not deplete.
The heat is sustained for quite a long time keeping the horse warm,
Makes sense to increase his hay rations at each approaching storm.

As the temperature drops, to stay warm more calories your horse burns,
More fiber generating heat makes both you and horse happy on your sojourns.
For temperature control make sure your horse's digestion is at its best,
Drinkable water is a must, not snow and ice so the horse is not distressed.
A horse will not stay properly hydrated if his water is icy and frozen,
Heat up the water a little so no ice is floating for the water to be chosen.

The more water you can get into a horse in the winter the better,
That way you can encourage him to drink more no matter the weather.
Provided they have some shelter, in winter horses can stay outdoors,
They actually prefer to remain outside in fresh air their health they restore.
With some protection like windbreaks, instead of seeking shelter in a barn,
They may choose to stand huddled together in the storm on the farm.

In winter it's better for horses if their shoes are not put on,
Since ice can form in the shoes making it hard for them to walk upon.
So very often for winter concerned horse owners may choose,
To make life easier for the horse by simply removing their horses shoes.
Whether barefoot or shod their hooves need regular care from the farrier,
Every six to eight weeks that visit makes them all the more merrier.

Looking after your horse involves daily lots of care and hard work,
Including watering, feeding, grooming and exercising but that's a perk.
Catching a problem early on before it become serieux is ideal,
Sickness, injury, weight loss, lost shoe, cracked hooves it helps to reveal.
First you yourself must stay warm, safe and be healthy yourself,
Because your horse is counting on you and he can't do it himself.

As I said before I had come all this way to see the land of snow,
And as a bonus all about taking care of horses I get to know.
GrandPere Anctil's hearty laugh promised adventure ahead,
Hesitating I thought that maybe I should have stayed in bed.
This bright sunny morning promised the day to be très beaux,
A parka, boots, scarf and furry mittens he made me wear before we go.

For me GrandPere took an extra blanket and a fur chapeau,
And we bravely proceeded out the door into the deep snow.
The wind had whistled and howled all through the night,
But now it was calm, the snow sparkly fresh and bright.
Yesterday the temperature I think was Celsius twenty two below,
GrandPere gave me earmuffs to put over those on my chapeau.

Today was warmer and it had snowed during the night,
Underfoot the snow was very crunchy sparkling and light.
Worried about my head being too hot GrandPere took off my hat,
He put on my head what looked like a sock with the word Labatt.
He said that it was traditional and he called it a tuque,
It had a large woolen pom, pom on it that always shook.

Travelling by sleigh in a village that time had forgot,
Under the sleigh blanket it was actually quite hot.
We glided past fields and lots and lots of trees,
Frost bite is a danger and exposed skin could freeze.
Like GrandPere I wrapped my scarf over my mouth,
Got attuned to the horse's rhythm and steam from his snout.

It's boules de neiges (snow ball) weather when it gets warmer,
The snow gets more moisture in it as if made to order.
For snow ball fights in school yards, pranks and for fun,
Making for merriment and playfulness quite a phenomenon.
Children make castles and bonne homme de neige, snowmen,
Some even dress them up as characters or businessmen.

It seemed much warmer in the woods among the many trees,
We came upon Emil and Felix, sons of Ambroise, at work in their chemise.
GrandPere knew both and the two sawing wood stopped to say bonjour,
They harvested arbres de noel (Christmas trees) to keep their business secure.
We passed their stockpile of Balsam fir, Scotch Pine, White Pine and Blue spruce,
And several others like Fraser fir and Korean fir they were proud to introduce.

Felix told us they export half of the harvest to the United States and Mexico,
And that is where they earn their pay and really make their dough.
He said in the market they are a primary producer of Christmas trees,
Balsam Fir the most popular Christmas tree they grow with ease.
They belong to the Quebec and CCTGA, the Canadian tree growers association,
That really help them with exporting a lot and they have good cooperation.

The trade groups for Christmas tree farmers were founded in 1972,
Beside exports they dealt with conservation and recycling issues really true.
Emil said that only about 20 percent of their crop is sold locally,
He wheezes and coughs but manages to say that boastfully.
This morning they had some problem with their tractor truck,
And brought it in to get fixed so they don't get stuck.

I wanted to get a feel of the green needles of the spruce,
And got my hand full of sap that would not come loose.
Working with Christmas trees can leave your hands sticky with sap,
Toothpaste or alcohol can dissolve the glue in a snap.
After exchanging pleasantries off we drove again,
GrandPere explained how these workmen were good handymen.

We arrived at the bank of the river all glacé in ice,
There in mid river stood gaily painted huts all very nice.
Some were being lived in since we saw chimney smoke,
He said they were ice fishing I thought it was a joke.
They make hole in the ice and use a short pole,
Sometime they catch much but they no can control.

Depends where they set up their hut and search,
Often catch good size pike, trout and lots of perch.
Jean Guy have Iroquois blood and know the place well,
He have very funny story that he like to often tell.
Americans they come their fishing luck to try,
Rent cabin set up real well and bait they over buy.

They fish, drink beer and in two days they catch none,
They think that its maybe better to cut their losses and run.
Jean Guy he come sit on the ice drill hole watched by everyone,
He is ten feet from them and pull out big fish one after one.
Americans come out scratch their heads wonder how it's perform,
Jean Guy laugh and tell them secret is to keep the worms warm.

Looks like he take out a big worm from out of his (mouth) bouche,
He wiggle it and throw it down the hole no let them even touche.
They beg and offer to buy his fish before he leave,
Deux cent piastres for his six fish he put up his sleeve.
He laugh and wonder how many worms they would eat,
Taking his gear he wish them good day a pleasure to meet.

For ice fishing you need a licence and some additional gear,
Like a heater, an auger, a scoop and lots of beer.
That's after you have a shelter so as not to freeze,
A rug to put over the ice and a blanket for up to your knees.
Some have small camp stove to cook their meal,
The challenge of catching fish has a very big appeal.

To pass the time a bunk bed or TV some find handy indeed,
And oh a warm toilet is most welcomed in time of need.
You can jig your short rod to catch the fish attention,
Up and down every few seconds without reservation.
Or use a tip up pole with a flag at the top,
When a fish bites the flag will pop up.

Most fishing will need minnows or live bait,
Best to use a plastic insulated cooler that's lightweight.
Don't forget to include a good net to get the minnow out,
Dipping your hands into frigid water make you cold throughout.
And include a simple towel to keep your hands dry,
It will help to protect your hands as many will testify.

Listen to the warning and always wear a flotation device,
In case you slip and fall under the ice to be very precise.
In the ice cold water remember your first priority is to get out fast,
Hypothermia could set in, you pass out and that breath is your last.
When you get out, quickly find shelter and some dry clothes,
Get something warm to drink and sit near a hot stove.

Jean Guy knew every duck pond, river and lake,
He even spoke to the fish and each snowflake.
He say, if deep enough these off the path nooks,
Led to some fine catches and loaded fish hooks.
You have to fish Tommy Cod called poulamon,

From early December to end of Février très bon.

Jean guy's friend Ti Jean, son of Aristide and Odette,
Both avid fishing guys clean fish like rolling a cigarette.
Ti Jean wear Kevlar glove to protect his hands from gills and fins,
And used a sharp fillet knife real quick as he grins.
They bring two gallons of spring water to rinse the fish,
Before they ready the fillets to be cooked and put on the dish.

Nothing taste better than fresh fish cooked on open fire,
After a great day a wonderful meal is all you require.
There is walleye, whitefish, trout, perch and pike,
They are fresh, and cooked they are sure to delight.
Ice fishing is quite boring if waiting until you freeze,
But enjoyable beyond your dreams as everyone agrees.

GrandPere told me a story and to this day I wonder if it's true,
But he delighted in telling it and he sure did laugh beaucoup.
Many here served as guides for tourists who would come to see,
Or to ice fish or take photos or enjoy the snow as happened to me.
They all left with fond memories of wonderful times spent well,
Leaving the people here with many great funny stories to tell.

Two touring guys walking in the snow, one was carrying their fishing gear,
Talking to each other, the other had his arms full carrying cases of beer.
The first one he say, " You got enough beer there it looks like for life,
With a sigh the second one say "Yeah! Well one case is for my wife.
The first one say, "I guess the trade you made was noble and worthwhile,
Confused the second one say "No that's in case she comes up here" with a smile.

Another story of two drunk guys in a hurry looking to fish through the ice,
See very big smooth and shiny ice field they think would be nice.
Kneeling, they take their small axes and strike the ice some hard blows,
"There's no fish under the ice" says a deep loud voice that knows,
They get scared and work harder look and seeing no one around,
Hearing the deep voice again they throw themselves to the ground.

Frustrated and very upset they chop and work faster and then,
"There's no fish under the ice" says the deep loud voice again.
One of them shouts back, "Who is talking to us?" an answer seeking,
The deep voice from above answers, "This is the Arena Manager speaking!"
They get up bewildered and their heads they are scratching,

They are told to sober up as the hole they made they will be patching.

Gilles, son of Gaspard and Manon like to travel, delivers Armand's homebrew,
He visit many auberge, lots of bars and places both old and new.
He never drink any liquor or hard stuff or even the odd beer,
Ever since he got terribly drunk and was very sick last year.
From his travels he always come back with lots of funny stories to tell,
He often entertain with his many episodes in Bastien's hotel.

In Montreal he saw same guy drinking heavy in every bar he go,
Gilles was not drinking he just enjoy visiting as we know.
One night he see the same guy lying in the street really drunk bad,
He check on him and find him alive and okay, he was really glad.
The guy kept repeating "It can't be done", Gilles don't know why,
The guy point to the sign, "Drink Canada Dry" which was overhead nearby.

Earlier GrandPere had attended to our horse with great care,
We bid our adieus as I struggled with my bulky outerwear.
Its late afternoon and the short days quite early are getting dark,
Once again into the sleigh, under the blankets it was time to embark.
"Attache ta tuque", said GrandPere as we slid along fast,
Along a windswept path of snow over the fields so vast.

Fish has always been an important subject in the area,
And has been reflected in the Catholic religion for millennia.
As par exemple all Fridays of the year are days of penance,
Abstaining from eating meat has been the normal stance.
Not having meat on Friday is reparation for our sins,
We make small sacrifice as the Church ordered when it begins.

Georges, son of Giles the barber, is a good hunter and loves barbeque,
He frequently bring home fresh venison, deer and caribou.
He cook outside and the aroma spreads into town real well,
And everyone know that Georges eating meat c'est pas nouvelle.
Every Friday the people smell George cooking and eating moose,
He is not supposed to, he sin and they don't know his excuse.

They complain to the Curée about George's big vice,

The Curée promise to talk to George the problem to stabilize.
Caught in the act Georges say he is not Catholic, now he protestant,
And that give him permission to eat meat whenever he want.
The Curée spend much time with Georges and they agree,
Before the people the Curée bless Georges again as Catholic for all to see.

The Curée sprinkle holy water on George make him wet really good,
He say, "You were protestant but now are Catholic". part of brotherhood,
George solemnly promised not to eat meat on Friday no more,
Come to church for a few weeks, his duty he did not ignore.
Then one Friday the people smelled the aroma of cooking moose,
Tell the Curée who go to see and find out what George's excuse.

Before speaking, the Curée watched George at the barbeque,
He sprinkle water on the meat and said as if right on cue.
"You were moose now you are fish", as the Curée had done,
The Curée was shocked and asked Georges what he had begun.
Seeing the Curée Georges said he was not going to eat moose,
And having fish on Friday was good, he had no excuse.

George told the Curée some interesting history from his research.
In the 17th century the Bishop of Quebec got permission from the church,
For his parishioners to eat beaver meat on Friday during lent.
The church declared beaver was a fish and he had their consent.
Maybe because the beaver was a good swimmer the church made the rule,
George asked the Curée if moose meat could be included without ridicule.

We don't know if Georges had more confession to make,
Or if absolution was even needed for George's sake.

Although Georges was cooking meat before the Curée put on the break,
George had the meat done but he did not eat or at all partake.
He cooked up and delivered to the church a lot of moose steak,
On Saturday they have town party giving everyone a bellyache.

GrandPere told me that Armand who makes his own booze,
Finds it hard to know why discouraging drinking booze the church choose.
After all it was monks who invented the apéritif Chartreuse,
For 200 years the monks made it and drank and were enthuse.
There is also Benedictine, Frangelico and Chateauneuf-de-Pape,
Monks were responsible for all the good stuff without much of a flap.

It was not only the evil of drinking that was condemned very strongly,
But the consequence of so doing and the terrible cost that we see.
Domestic trouble, children without clothes, food or shoes in the snow,
Families destitute and broken apart with a drunk husband that everyone know.
It's the welfare of the community that gives the church great concern,
Our saintly fathers warn us about pleasures of the flesh that we yearn.

Included in these admonishments dancing was called the ruin of souls,
Mothers were advised to teach their daughters modesty, shame and controls.
To set proper goals, promote good morals and to teach chastity,
Not to make spectacles of themselves with cosmetics, indecent clothing and sensuality.
Women were warned not to invite others to sin not by words but by how they dress,
Their behaviour made others sin in their hearts so they were accountable nonetheless.

Confession is compulsory and absolution was not automatically given,
Not all father confessors were understanding and not all sins were forgiven.
Some people had to search for easygoing priests whom to consult,
Many lived in sin and did even worse feeling there was no way out, as a result.
News of finding an understanding priest quickly was spread around,
And many found absolution and salvation making life changes very profound.

GrandPere said that before 1965 all masses were in Latin celebrated,
It was only after the Second Vatican Council that local language mass was officiated.
We heard Dominus Vobiscum (The Lord be with you) blessing used by the Curée,
In 2007 Pope Benedict's decree called for wider use of Latin mass today.
Many traditionalists cheered and many bishops were opposed,
Many priests no longer knew how and so were exposed.

We passed over several ponts couverts (covered bridges) on our way,
Built from the late 1800s right up to 1950 they stood with no decay.
The Quebec Ministry of Colonization adopted them as their favourite design,
And built them real solid, aesthetically pleasing and they work fine.
In winter with no bridge people waited for the river to freeze,
Or they used a time consuming ferry or barge to attend to their needs.

I actually made many trips with GrandPere over several days being away,
But I wrote the adventures here as occurring on the same day.
It gives the impression of very long days with excitement filled,
Which more accurately portrays the moments my dreams were fulfilled.
Seeing, speaking and participating with people all as busy as can be,
Tending to their chores their livelihood taking time to spend with me.

GrandPere told me how in his youth he and others worked with their parents,
Hunting, fishing, haymaking, milking, stable work and running errands.
When they were a little older they used to have house dances,

With people packed into one room it was hot under the circumstances.
But it was fun and those dances had many toe tapping fiddlers,
Whole families played the violin so they had many contributors.

That was the only musical instrument other than the organ that they had,
But the organ, you couldn't move from house to house too bad.
That's how it was until Rene bring his accordion, Luc his guitar,
The news spread and people attended from near and from afar.
The violin and accordion are the instruments most used in traditional Quebec music.
First and foremost it is danse music and is very therapeutic.

The repertoire was built by generations of musicians mostly all by ear,
From each other or their parents based on what they hear.
Also often used is the harmonica called "musique à bouche",
Because of its portability and giving the tunes a warm touche.
The harmonica is used for dances such as reels and "gigues" (jigs) at a soiree,
Most musicians learned the tunes by ear sitting on their father's knee.

The harmonica with fiddle in Quebec music is often portrayed,
It often accompanies the fiddle and accordion but is also solo played.
The accordion was invented in Austria in 1829, eighteen twenty nine,
In 1843 the Ursuline convent of Quebec bring the first one to Quebec, very fine.
in 1895 Odilon Gagné got his accordion manufacturing business in Quebec underway,
The company, Maison Gagné et frères is still in business today.

The one-row diatonic ten button accordion are the ones,
That we happily play and which we use to teach our sons.
Just like the very first accordions that were brought here,
It plays like a harmonica but with bellows to be clear.
In Quebec music, the fiddle, accordion and harmonica are well respected
And played together at house parties they are well connected.

The fiddle or violin came to Quebec in the mid-1600s and is most commonly used,
And the two words fiddle and violin same thing are often are confused.
The fiddle is key for Quebec's traditional music and vibrant culture,

Fiddle music has been used to energize and socialize and helps to endure.
The fiddle stands for family, for tradition, for the working class and for status,
Expressing every feeling of the human heart that we can discuss.

Fiddles are a strong connection to our traditions and our past,
There is a vast repertoire of chansons and tunes that we have amassed.
Québécois music is full of life and part of the national identity,
It was clear early on that dancing and fiddling were the people's specialty.
The Québec fiddle has a distinctive rhythm and joie-de-vivre,
That is always greatly admired and enjoyed by the receiver.

An early solo fiddler with La Famille Soucy was Isidore Soucy (1899-1963),
His well attended performances were always filled with joy and lots of esprit.
In the early 1960s he was popular, "Chez Isidore" was his TV show,
He was well known as a Québécois fiddler, he get many awards, très beau.
Dances like the quadrille, the polka and waltz were brought from Europe one assumes,
This included the gigue (jig), traditional stepdancing, which inspired a host of tunes.

Most are accompanied by a distinct and wonderful loud foot tapping sound,
Keeping the fiddlers' feet energetically going all the time on the ground.
We have many chansons à réponse (call-and-response) songs which shine,
Many of these songs come from before the colonization of the New World time.
Many were brought over by the colonists and voyageurs,
Get transferred here when they work to export the furs.

Chansons à réponse involve verses by a lead singer and choruses repeated,
By a group of singers over and over until the song is completed.
Borrowing existing tunes and replacing lyrics is nothing new,
Lyrics are usually of the singer's own composition and are mieux beaucoup.
As songs were passed on through oral tradition, people added their own texts,
With regional stories or familiar local phrases, giving the tune their own effects.

At the time the presence of violins in Québec's were met with indignation,
The church held that fiddles and dancing, were tools of evil deserving condemnation.
The priests attempted to banish the music and debauchery with brimstone and fire,
They objected to music and dancing believing it led to drinking and desire.
They regarded the fiddle as the instrument of the devil,
And threatened fiddlers with hell and from church to expel.

Slowly the churches views changed to tolerance, acceptance, and finally endorsement,
Perhaps the financial resources reaped from parish picnics helped the reinforcement.
By the mid 1900s to encourage fiddle music and dancing at picnics the priests chose,
They even initiated concerts of singing, fiddling and step dancing at these shows.
The church recognized the important role of music and dancing in maintaining morale,
And that was throughout the entire region not only in the general locale.

In small communities the priest always have lots of power and make a big impact,
They said that the only proper attitude to drink was total abstinence to be exact.
In the community the priests' influence extended far and wide,
Basically the priests laid down the law and everyone complied.
But a few abused their power when they dominated community life,
And shamed people threatening hell and damnation in the afterlife.

In most cases priests have had a really progressive positive impact,
Even promoting and participating in music and dancing as a matter of fact.
How priests influenced their parishioners differed in their interventions,
Eliciting supportive cooperation or contributed to emotional tensions.
The parish priest is considered a religious leader and everyday advisor,
People always preferred the sympathizer, organizer and harmonizer.

Priests took part in politics, economics, culture and religion every day,
And through his homilies and conduct public opinion he did sway.
Some were social advocates and others were strict disciplinarians,
Some were young inexperienced and others were septuagenarians.
Priests created legal documents, made recommendations and settled disputes,
Normally associated with elected officials were such attributes.

The family was and is very nurturing and a strong unit of society,
The village has a good variety with people sharing piety and sobriety.
The village is a tightly knit community and everybody knows everyone,
Music and dancing bring more freedom, joy, gaiety and good fun.
It helps people to expel anxiety through fiddling and song very energetic,
They forget their troubles empathize and become more sympathetic.

GrandPere said, When the ice on the river was thick enough to haul wood with no fears,
The river became their skating and hockey rink where many started their careers.
They played hockey right up until the ice started to crack and melt,
Of friends and neighbours they made up hockey teams to play whenever they felt.
Because of their complaints a separate rink for the girls to skate was built,
That way the boys could play hockey without constraint or feeling any guilt.

Fathers and sons made up the teams for a little game between friends,
Each one played as hard as if they were in the NHL they pretend.
GrandPere remembered one time when they lost the puck,
It flew down the rink and it was gone into the water 'pluck'.
They found some merde (horse manure) frozen solid of course,
And continued to play with much enthusiasm and force.

Henri, son of Alphonse the inventor, made a break and went flying down the ice,
With the manure puck going straight towards his father, the goalie to be precise.

Alphonse, yelled out as loud as he could, 'Don't shoot Henri! Don't shoot!'
Henri slap shot hit that manure with all his might it was too late to reroute.
It knock the pipe from Alphonse's mouth with a smack, make him very mad,
Imagine getting a face full of frozen merde (horse manure) very sad.

Henri, red faced started running for his life with his father after him,
Both of them not good at running with skates on, they kept falling pretty grim.
Henri's team won but all the way home Henri he run breathing hard,
He promised his father 's advice he would never again disregard.
They had used that manure patty as a puck pretty much all of that game,
Everyone feel sorry for Henri funniest thing they could not blame.

Was it okay to have father and son on opposing team not to be outdone,
The question was long debated and was the talk of the town.
Some people after see Alphonse searching for his pipe all over the place,
They long remember him splattered with merde on his face.
Maybe Alphonse got a brand new pipe that day,
Because people still saw him smoking anyway.

GrandPere stopped by a cabane à sucre (sugar shack) when he saw two guys wave,
They both laugh as we very much surprised behave.
They are Anselme and Aristide, own a cabane and many maple trees,
They are outside smoking, taking a break, enjoying the breeze.
Both of them are maple syrup producers which is quite an art,
GrandPere knew them a long time right from the start.

They were just planning and tending to the maple tree grove,
And invited us into the cabane to warm up and sit by the stove.
I took the opportunity to ask them about their endeavour,
And they freely discussed business with us with great allure.
To produce maple syrup they use the sap from three species of maple trees,
The sugar maple, the black maple and the red maple best in the diocese.

Because of the high sugar content in the sap of two to five percent,
Early budding in the season alters the flavour of the sap they lament.
They basically own and operate a maple syrup production farm,
It takes a lot of work but they have been inventive giving it more charm.

Their cabane à sucre louvered at the top had a window which opened in a snap,
Which was used to vent the steam from the hot boiling sap.

I learned a great deal as they talked with much expertise,
It took much labour to tap the trees and boil the sap with ease.
Between them they have fourteen children, eleven who help very well,
In springtime they all worked hard and have stories to tell.
All the equipment, pails, troughs (spigots), kettles and such they share,
In summer they cut wood and stored it at the shack with no space to spare.

After collecting and bringing the sap to the shack, it is boiled,
In a large kettle to get it to be a syrup long days have they toiled.
Maple syrup when judged ready, carefully into barrels is poured,
Then it is sold in bulk or shipped close to home where it is stored.
It is also poured into smaller containers and different shaped bottles,
And is sold at open air farmer markets, grocery stores and hotels.

Maples are not tapped until they are 30 to 40 years old,
Until they are over 100 years old they can continue to produce gold.
The tree trunk diameter determines whether we use one to three tap,
Each season an average maple tree will produce 35 to 50 litres of sap.
That is very roughly about up to 12 litres of sap every day,
Mother Nature determines how much sap flow and how much stay.

From March to Mid April the season lasts four to eight weeks,
We have to work quick and use good production techniques.
In the 1970s a large number of technological changes took place,
Plastic tubing was installed to collect the sap many pails we replace.

We add pumps and even preheaters to recycle heat lost in the steam,
Machines to remove water before boiling the sap were added to the scheme.

Collected sap must be boiled down to obtain maple syrup pure,
Takes about 35 volumes of sap boiled to get 1 volume of syrup for sure.
Boiling is a tightly controlled process, to ensure sugar content is perfect,
Boiled too long or too short affects the quality and will be reject.
You get one gallon of syrup from 57 gallons of 1.5% sugar content sap,
But you only need 25 gallons of 3.5% sugar content sap, a big handicap.

The filtered syrup is graded and packaged while still hot,
Into metal, glass, or coated plastic containers right on the spot.
We also boil the syrup longer to make other products very classy,
Including maple sugar, maple butter or cream, and maple candy or taffy.
There are several cabanes à sucre (sugar shacks) to be found,
Come spring, syrup lovers by the hundreds come around.

After a long and arduous winter they occupy all the cabane seats,
To eat and drink and very much enjoy the sticky sweet maple treats.
In the "cozy cabin décor," a menu of traditional dishes to them appeals,
They sit at long communal tables and simply enjoy maple-laden meals.
Welcoming spring, simple sugar shack food includes delicious hot pea soup,
Baked beans, meat pie, omelette and maple sugar pie is served to the group.

Steamy bowls of pea soup, (Soupe aux pois) with homemade bread are a big hit,
Drizzled with maple syrup with bread and butter it's fantastic you must admit.
Pancakes with maple syrup, maple-wood smoked trout and meatball stew,
Along with fried pork rinds (oreilles de crisse), which everyone likes beaucoup.
Devilled eggs with maple smoked sugar-cured ham and sugar pie,
Pork confit tourtière drizzled with more maple syrup meant to satisfy.

Dumplings in maple syrup, bread pudding, homemade sausage and waffles,
Aristide, Anselme and servers run around, everyone's satisfaction they ensures.

Dessert has more goodies even a giant puff pastry with maple whipped cream,
And pineapple poutine and the classic maple taffy on snow what a dream.
Their description worked up quite the voracious appetite in me,
And built up a tremendous respect for the great maple tree.

We thanked them for building up our expectation for spring,
We left promising to return so that we would not miss anything.
We continued on our voyage and saw many decorated Christmas trees,
Warm in the sleigh. the bells on our horse rang out merrily in the breeze.
We were approaching the festival of Christmas a time of good cheer,
And soon we would be chasing out the old and welcoming in a happy new year.

We had great experiences, met wonderful people wherever we roam,
I was surprised to suddenly see familiar places we were closer to home.
We stopped near Ambroise's home, a Christmas tree plot,
With old Amboise tending shop, he was helping his sons we thought.
We told him that we had met Emil and Felix harvesting trees,
Even now as the temperature had dropped several degrees.

Ambroise said that their tractor truck had broken down,
And that they hauled it to Gaston's garage closer in town.
He said that with horses they would have had better luck,
Rather than feeding gas and oil and have repairs on the truck.
GrandPere told him not to despair they would be home soon,
Ambroise sure hoped so because he missed his nap this afternoon.

We came to Gaston, son of Florent, the forgeron in town,
Gaston was mécanicien with excellent reputation renown.
He had just finished work on Emil and Felix tractor truck,
Proudly he showed off his handiwork amid all the muck.
He was going to drive out and help the boys load those trees,
He loaded the truck with hot soup and whatever he could seize.

It was getting cold, we wished him well and got ourselves under way,
We crawled under the blankets to keep warm in our sleigh.
GrandPere had looked after the horse having watered and fed him well,
We passed places with Christmas trees decorated as best as we could tell.
It was getting much darker now and light reflected from the glistening snow,
We made a swooshing sound as we glided along it was très beaux.

GrandPere said, "We have two game nights happening here per week,
They provide great social interaction a social highlight that people seek".
A fun evening with friends the card games get people talking,
While the game play is often very thought-provoking.
Games are played with "relegation" and "promotion" among the tables,
At each table the winner moving "up" and the loser moving "down" when able.

Often at the table people have food, drink and such,
We don't worry about cataclysmic spillage too much.
Players talk about things other than what's going on in the game,
It's a great way to unwind, relax and have fun all the same.
It's a time to forget about commitments and work and to focus on play,
The point of the activity is to enjoy yourself passing the time away.

Game nights started years ago in different rotating homes,
We quickly run out of space with many disappointed groans.
Next came the hotel and finally to the centre d'Accueil community centre,
Big enough space but get full up real fast when we enter.
Play adds joy to life and connects you to others around you,
Playing with family and friends helps relieve stress and depression too.

The games promote an overall sense of well-being, temporarily relieve pain,
They help you adapt, improve memory and problem solve, challenge the brain.
Sharing laughter, gossip, heart aches, jokes and fun is a fantastic therapy,
To increase friendship, compassion, trust, intimacy and empathy,
It helps you overcome all forms of aggravations with practicality,

And it boosts your energy and vitality with a dose of reality.

We play with standard 52 playing cards (jeu de cartes),
Some know all the tricks and rules and can play really smart.
The cards are the same with pictures each game it enlivens,
In French the suits are trèfles (clubs♣), carreaux (diamonds♦),
And of course cœurs (hearts♥), and piques (spades♠).
In every known game that is played the suit pervades.

At every single table a deck of cards is used and voila,
Each suit has the valet (jack), the dame (queen), and the (king) roi.
We have people playing Charlemagne a variant of bid euchre at a table,
The rules are intricate and are hard to master but somehow they are able.
To play they must make sure to use all their brains for that game,
Sometime they mix up the rules and each other they blame.

We play two Hundred (Deux Cents), La Bloutte, La Fouine or Le Ruff,
Many versions are easy to learn but there are many that are tough.
We also play Trou du cul (Asshole) also called Rich Man Poor Man,
For that one you need watch careful and a good attention span.
We also play the game 500 (Cinq Cents) with a 46-card pack,
Throwing out the twos and threes and adding two jokers back.

Dame de pique (a French version of Hearts) is also played,
Often thoughtful and sometimes foolish moves are made.
They play different rules and know which illegal moves they make,
Some mistakes give all the players a big bad headache.
In every different game, cards may have different ranks,
That opens the game for players having different pranks.

Another French Canadian game is (Mittens) Mitaines,
Everybody keeps points score on paper using their pens.
Points are scored for sets of two equal ranked cards, played to the discard pile,
All while chatting or snacking or smiling making it all worthwhile.
Two equal cards are a mitaine (mitten), three cards are a gant (glove),
And four cards are a chausson (sock), complex rule thank God above.

You can capture the discard pile by matching the top card or playing a jack,
The cards that do not form mittens, gloves or socks into the pile you put back.
Games like La Politaine (or Les Quatre Sept), or La Poule are also played,
Along with many games I don't even know their names I'm afraid.

When the people play they talk and many stories they tell,
Last week we hear a story that make us all laugh very well.

In a nearby town lived Alain and Yvette,
Rumour had it that she was easy to get.
Pierre and Simone were playing cards with them,
When Pierre's card fell under the table close to the femme.
Pierre crawled under the table, his card to retrieve,
And saw a sight he could hardly believe.

Yvette was sitting sans culottes with legs apart,
Pierre lingered awhile finding it hard to depart.
The card game they all continued to play,
Later alone in the kitchen to Pierre Yvette would say.
Under the table did you enjoy the view?
Pierre nodded pouring himself some home brew.

Yvette said for cent piastres you could have a sample,
Whenever Alain is not home for example.
Days later Pierre showed up money in hand,
Retiring to the bedroom it all went as planned.
Pierre left satisfied before Alain got home,
He even had time to shower and comb.

Arriving Alain asked if Pierre had come by today,
If she received 100 piastres that he had to pay.

She surprised said yes, why do you ask, mon amour,
This morning I lent him the money to be repaid for sure.
I'm happy to have such a trustworthy friend and true,
One who keeps his word mon petit chou.

We arrived at the centre d'Accueil where fiddle music was heard,
In we went and saw musicians and dancers who swirled.
I noted male dancers in black pants, white shirts with red sashes swinging,
And I admired some very pretty girls standing and singing.
I saw fast footwork with spurts of aggressive energy thrown in,
The music came from marvellously played accordion and violin.

They have a dance called gigue (step dance) GrandPere told me,
Amazed by the rhythmic sound of fiddles and tapping feet fast as can be.
The dancers had shoes with metal taps at the toe and heel,
Each one had developed steps to the music they did feel.
Gigue (jig) dancing is a unique art needing very little space,
The lively fiddle music putting a smile on the energetic dancers face.

The gigue had its origin in the lumber camps and is danced alone,
The lumbermen passed their leisure time dancing and thinking of home.
For the gigue in Quebec at a soiree there is no substitute,
For the energy expelled the joy and excitement is absolute.
The gigue is played in 2/4 and 3/2 time and is very fast,
The diversion in the cold wintertime is unsurpassed.

GrandPere said beside this solo dance they enjoy the swing,
The reel is for men and women more a social thing.
The couples twirl round and around on the floor,

People are happy and animated as never before.
Dancing to reels are the most popular one,
It is played in 4/4 time, is very lively, fast and full of fun.

Another dance they do well is the quadrille,
Being aware of one's partner takes lots of skill.
People just overjoyed to be dancer and danseuse,
Happy tapping together with their shoes if they so choose.
Here was the essence of country music a la Quebecois,
Energetic, foot tapping, joie de vivre music filled with awe.

Several fiddlers with violins held close to the chin,
Each with both legs tapping to the rhythm thrown in.
GrandPere said that some of the priests in the not too distant past,
Were very strict insisting on no music or dancing would be aghast.
The actual Christmas season was Christmas eve until Epiphany,
Delaying any celebrations until after Midnight Mass with their rigidity.

The current Curée have no strong opinion seem to be okay,
But publicly to the old timers we think he look the other way.
Practicing also was the assembled group choir who desired,
Simply to harmonize and sing together and to be admired.
Among them was a frequent participant as church soloist,
With the music they had fun but come for practise they insist.

There is a song "Swing la bacaisse" that people sing and dance to,
That is often performed, is very popular and liked beaucoup.
To the Québécois the term bacaisse defines a woman of large size.
One with a large bottom, big belly and fat thighs.
Swing refers to dance and a coffin is symbolized by the wooden box,
The expression make a big woman dance to exhaustion right off her socks,

SWING LA BACAISSE dans le fond de la boîte à bois
Swing the bacaisse into the bottom of the wooden box

French	English Translation
Paroles de Swing La Bacaisse	The words of Swing Bacaisse
Swigne la bacaisse dans le fond de la boîte à bois.	Swing the bacaisse in the bottom of the wooden box.
Tout le monde balance et pis	Everyone swings and everyone

tout le monde danse. Tout le monde est malheureux tout seul dans sa bulle. On pense qu`on avance, moi je pense qu`on recule. On danse pis on dépense notre pécule comme une gang de barbares accrochés au bar. Des pitounes et des pétards, tout le monde sur le radar. Tout le monde se croit pis ça cruise en criant. « Hey, je t`ai-tu déjà vu à la T.V? »	dances. Everyone is unhappy alone in his bubble. We think we're advancing, I think we're going backwards. We dance and spend our nest egg like a gang Of barbarians clinging to the bar. Pitons and firecrackers, everyone on the radar. Everyone thinks it worse that crushes by shouting. "Hey, have you seen me on TV?" "
Swigne la bacaisse dans le fond de la boîte à bois.	Swing the bacaisse in the bottom of the wooden box.
Les femmes au milieu les hommes autour. C'est une mascarade le grand jeu de l`amour. Si je te paye une ligne vas-tu me dire bonjour? « Si t`as un char c`est avec toi que je pars! Pis ôte ta capine. Veux-tu jouer de ma mandoline? Pis rentre dans ma chambre et pis commence à t`étendre. Pis ôte ton jupon que je te swigne le madelon.	The women in the middle the men around. It is a masquerade the great game of love. If I pay you a line will you say hello? "If you have a chariot with you I'm going!" " And take off your cap. Would you play my mandolin? And it goes back to my room and it begins to stretch. And take off your petticoat so that I could swing you the madelon.
Trois petits coups tu t`en retournes chez vous...	Three small shots you go back home ...
Swigne la bacaisse dans le fond de la boîte à bois.	Swing the bacaisse in the bottom of the wooden box.
Stop! Changez de côté vous vous êtes trompés!	Stop! Change the side you have made a mistake!
On oublie les discothèques et pis les cruising bars... On va se louer toute la gang un petit shack dans le nord... Un violon, deux guitares, pis des bouteilles de fort en masse On va fêter le fait qu`on est pas encore mort...	We forget the nightclubs and the cruising bars We will rent all the gang a little shack in the north ... A violin, two guitars, worse bottles of fort en masse We're going to celebrate the fact that we're not dead yet ...

French	English Translation
(On est-y mort?)	(Are we dead?)
On va se conter des histoires de démons pis d`esprits...	We are going to tell stories of demons and worse spirits
On va bourrer nos pipes d`herbe du pays...	We're going to stuff our grass pipes ...
Ô canabis, herbe de nos aïeux...	O canabis, grass of our ancestors ...
le monde est bien plus beau assis autour d`un feu...	The world is much more beautiful sitting around a fire ...
Regardez dans le ciel... La lune nous sourit...	Look in the sky ... The moon smiles at us ...
Tout le monde dans le lac pour un bain de minuit!	Everyone in the lake for a midnight swim!
Swigne la bacaisse dans le fond de la boîte à bois.	Swigne the bacaisse in the bottom of the wooden box.

PRENDRE UN VERRE DE BIÈRE MON MINOU

French	English Translation
Prendre un verre de bière mon minou	Take a glass of beer my minou
Prendre un verre de bière right through	Take a glass of beer right through
Tu prends ta bière	You take your beer
Tu m'en donnes pas	You do not give me any
Je te fais des belles façons	I make beautiful ways for you
Je te chante des belles chansons	I sing beautiful songs for you
Donne moi en donc	Give me some then

LES FRAISES ET LES FRAMBOISES; (Strawberries and Raspberries;)

French	English Translation
Sur la route de Longueuil	On the road to Longueuil
De Longueuil à Chambly	From Longueuil to Chambly
J'ai rencontré trois beaux	I met three beautiful
Trois beaux gars du pays	Three beautiful guys from the country
J'ai fait risette au jeune	I made the young man laugh
C'était le plus joli	It was the nicest
Il me clignait de l'œil	He winked at me
En me disant ceci	In telling me this
Ah les fraises et les framboises	Ah strawberries and raspberries
Du bon vin j'en ai bu	Good wine I have drank
Croyez-moi, chers villageois	Believe me, dear villagers
Jamais je me suis tant plu	Never have I liked so much

Il me clignait de l'œil	He winked at me
En me disant ceci	In telling me this
Venez, donc cher ami	Come, then dear friend
Y'en a encore a boire	There's still some more to drink
Venez, donc cher ami	Come, then dear friend
Y en a encore à boire	There's still some more to drink
Venez, donc cher ami	Come, then dear friend
Y en a encore à boire	There's still some more to drink
Ah les fraises et les framboises	Ah strawberries and raspberries
Du bon vin j'en ai bu	Good wine I have drank
Croyez-moi, chers villageois	Believe me, dear villagers
Jamais je me suis tant plu	Never have I liked so much

YOUPE! YOUPE! SUR LA RIVIÈRE

French	English translation:
Par un dimanche au soir, M'en allant promener	One Sunday night we went walking,
Et moi et puis François, tous deux de compagnie	My friend François and me to find some company
Chez le bonhomme' Gauthier on est allé veiller	A visit we made to old bonhomme Gauthier
Je vais vous raconter l'tour qui m'est arrivé.	I'll tell you just what happened to me next,
REFRAIN	CHORUS
Youpe! Youpe! sur la rivière	Youpe! Youpe! on the river..
Vous ne m'entendez guère	You can hardly hear me
Youpe! Youpe! sur la rivière	Youpe! Youpe! on the river..
Vous ne m'entendez pas	You don't hear me at all.
J'y allumai ma pipe, comme' c'était la façon,	I lit up my pipe, as it was customary to do
Disant quelques paroles aux gens de la maison	speaking a few words to the people of the house.
Je dis à Délima: "Me permettriez-vous	I said to Délima "Would you permit me
De m'éloigner des autres pour m'approcher de vous?"	to come aside, so that I could approach you alone?"
REFRAIN	CHORUS
Ah! oui, vraiment, dit-elle, avec un grand plaisir	"Ah, yes," she said, "with great pleasure.
Tu es venu ce soir, c'est seulement pour un rire.	You came here tonight just for fun;
Tu es trop infidèle pour me parler d'amour:	you are too unfaithful to speak to me of love.
T'as la P'tit Jérémie que tu aimes toujours."	It is your little Jérémie you always love."

REFRAIN

Revenons au bonhomme' qu'est dans lit, couché
Criant à haute voix: "Lima, va te coucher!
   Les gens de la compagne, des villes et des faubourgs
   Retirez-vous d'ici, car il fait bientôt jour!"

REFRAIN

J'n'attends pas qu'on m'l dise pour la seconde fois,
Et je dis à François: "T'en viens-tu quand et moi?
Bonsoir, ma Délima, je file mon chemin!"
Je m'en allais nu-tête, mon chapeau à la main

REFRAIN

CHORUS

Let us get back to the old man, who was in bed asleep.
He cried loudly, "Lima! Go to bed!
People of the country, towns and outskirts,
Leave because it's getting late. It will soon be day."

CHORUS

I didn't wait to be told a second time.
And I said to François, "Are you coming with me?
Good night my Délima, I'll be on my way
I left with my head uncovered, my hat in my hand.

CHORUS

C'EST L'AVIRON

French
M'en revenant de la jolie Rochelle;
J'ai rencontré trois jolies demoiselles.

REFRAIN
C'est l'aviron qui nous mène, qui nous mène
C'est l'aviron qui nous mène en haut!

J'ai rencontré trois jolies demoiselles
J'ai point choisi, mai j'ai pris la plus belle.

REFRAIN

J'ai point choisi, mai j'ai pris la plus belle
J'l'y fis monter derrièr' moi, sur

English Translation:
Returning from Rochelle

I encountered three pretty young ladies.

CHORUS
It's the rowing that takes us

It's the rowing that takes us to the high country

I encountered three pretty young ladies.
I chose the prettiest,

CHORUS

I chose the prettiest,

who got on my saddle behind

ma selle.

REFRAIN

J'l'y fis monter derrièr' moi, sur ma selle
J'y fis cent lieues sans parler avec elle.

REFRAIN

J'y fis cent lieues sans parler avec elle
Au bout d'cent lieues, ell' me d'mandit à boire.

REFRAIN

Au bout d'cent lieues, ell'me d'mandit à boire
Je l'ai menée auprès d'une fontaine.

REFRAIN

Je l'ai menée auprès d'une fontaine
Quand ell' fut là, ell' ne voulut point boire.

REFRAIN

Quand ell' fut là, ell' ne voulut point boire
Je l'ai menée au logis de son père.

REFRAIN

Je l'ai menée au logis de son père
Quand ell' fut là, ell' buvait à pleins verres.

REFRAIN

Quand ell' fut là, ell' buvait à pleins verres
À la Santé de son père et sa mère.

me.

CHORUS

who got on my saddle behind me.
We rode one hundred leagues without talking

CHORUS

We rode one hundred leagues without talking
until she asked for a drink.

CHORUS

until she asked for a drink.
I took her to a spring,

CHORUS

I took her to a spring,
where she refused to drink.

CHORUS

where she refused to drink.
I took her to her father's home,

CHORUS

I took her to her father's home,
Where she drank glass after glass

CHORUS

Where she drank glass after glass
And toasted to the health Of her mother and father,

REFRAIN

À la Santé de son père et sa mère
À la Santé de ses soeurs et ses frères.

REFRAIN

À la Santé de ses soeurs et ses frères
À la Santé d' celui que son coeur aime.

REFRAIN

CHORUS

And toasted to the health Of her mother and father,
Her sisters and brothers

CHORUS

Her sisters and brothers

And the one she loved.

CHORUS

A LA CLAIRE FONTAINE

French
A la claire fontaine, m'en allant promener,
J'ai trouvé l'eau si belle que je m'y suis baigné.

REFRAIN
Il y a longtemps que je t'aime,

Jamais je ne t'oublirai,

Sous les feuilles d'un chêne, je me suis fait sécher.
Sur la plus haute branche, un rossignol chantait.

REFRAIN

Chante, rossignol, chante, toi qui as le coeur gai.
Tu as le coeur à rire, moi je l'ai-t-à pleurer.

REFRAIN

J'ai perdu ma maitresse sans l'avoir mérité.
Pour un bouquet de roses que je lui refusai.

REFRAIN

English Translation:
I was walking by a clear fountain
And the water was so inviting that I took a swim.

CHORUS
For a long time I have loved you,
Never will I forget you."

I dried myself under an oak tree
and heard a nightingale singing on the top branch.

CHORUS

"Sing, nightingale, you have a happy heart.
Your heart is laughing and mine is crying.

CHORUS

I lost my love, without deserving to,
because I refused her a bouquet of roses.

CHORUS

Je voudrais que la rose fût encore au rosier.
Et moi et ma maîtresse dans les mêm's amitiés.

I wish the rose was still on the bush
and that she and I still had the same affections.

CHEVALIERS DE LA TABLE RONDE

French
Chevaliers de la table ronde,
Goûtons voir si le vin est bon.

English Translation:
Knights of the round table,
let us drink to see if he wine is good.

Chevaliers de la table ronde,
Goûtons voir si le vin est bon.

Knights of the round table,
let us drink to see if he wine is good.

Goûtons voir, oui, oui, oui,
Goûtons voir, non, non, non,
Goûtons voir si le vin est bon.

let us drink to see, yes, yes, yes
let us drink to see, no, no, no
let us drink to see if he wine is good.

J'en boirai cinq a six bouteilles,
une femme sur mes genoux.
J'en boirai cinq a six bouteilles,
une femme sur mes genoux.
une femme, oui, oui, oui
une femme, non, non, non
une femme sur mes genoux.

I would drink five or six bottles with a woman on my knee.
I would drink five or six bottles with a woman on my knee.
with a woman, yes, yes, yes
with a woman, no, no, no
with a woman on my knee.

S'il est bon, s'il est agréable,

If the wine is good, if it is agreeable,

J'en boirai jusqu`à mon plaisir
S'il est bon, s'il est agréable,

I would drink to my pleasure.
If the wine is good, if it is agreeable,

J'en boirai jusqu`à mon plaisir
J'en boirai oui, oui, oui,
J'en boirai, non, non, non,
J'en boirai jusqu`'à mon plaisir.

I would drink to my pleasure.
I would drink, yes, yes, yes
I would drink, no, no, no
I would drink to my pleasure

Si je meurs, je veux qu'on m'enterre
Dans une cave où il y a du bon vin.
Sie je meurs, je veux qu'on m'enterre
Dans une cave où il y a du bon vin.
Dans une cave oui, oui, oui,
Dans une cave non, non, non,
Dans une cave où il y a du bon vin.

If I die, I want to be interred
in a cave where there is good wine.
If I die, I want to be interred
in a cave where there is good wine.
in a cave, yes, yes, yes
in a cave, no, no, no
in a cave where there is good wine.

Les deux pieds contre la muraille

My two feet against the wall

Et la tête sous le robinet.	and my head under the spigot.
Les deux pieds contre la muraille	My two feet against the wall
Et la tête sous le robinet.	and my head under the spigot.
Et la tête oui, oui, oui,	and my head, yes, yes, yes
Et la tête non, non, non,	and my head, no, no, no
Et la tête sous le robinet.	and my head under the spigot.
Et si le tonneau se débouche,	And if the cask flows,
J'en boirai jusqu'à mon loisir.	I would drink at my leisure.
Et si le tonneau se débouche,	And if the cask flows,
J'en boirai jusqu'à mon loisir.	I would drink at my leisure.
J'en boirai, oui, oui, oui,	I would drink, yes, yes, yes
J'en boirai, non, non, non,	I would drink, no, no, no
J'en boirai jusqu'à mon loisir.	I would drink at my leisure.
Sur ma tombe je veux qu'on inscrive:	On my tomb I wish one would write,
"Ici gît le roi des buveurs".	"Here lies the king of drinkers."
Sur ma tombe je veux qu'on inscrive:	On my tomb I wish one would write,
"Ici gît le roi des buveurs".	"Here lies the king of drinkers."
Ici gît, oui, oui, oui,	Here lies, yes, yes, yes
Ici gît, non, non, non,	Here lies, no, no, no
Ici gît le roi des buveurs	"Here lies the king of drinkers."

We enjoyed the music the singing and dancing while we stayed
There were many other toe tapping tunes that they played
Among them were:

Le quadrille de Rivière-du-Loup;	Quadrille de Gaspé; Paul Jones
Le réel de Ste-Anne;	La bastringue;
La guenille;	Les noces d'argent;
Le réel de Sherbrooke;	Le coq sur la clôture;
Réel de la Pointe-au-Pic;	La belle Québécoise;

Je porte un toast, je lève mon verre,
Au bon vieux temps qu'on se rappelle.
A mes chère amies, et a GrandPere,
Je porte un toast, je lève mon verre.
I salute the sweet wholesome sirop d'érable,
I want to return for it and a maple sugar slab.

I propose a toast, I raise my glass.
To the good old days we remember.

To my dear friends, and to GrandPere,
I propose a toast, I raise my glass.
This is my best Christmas I do declare,
And I'll forever keep you in my prayer.

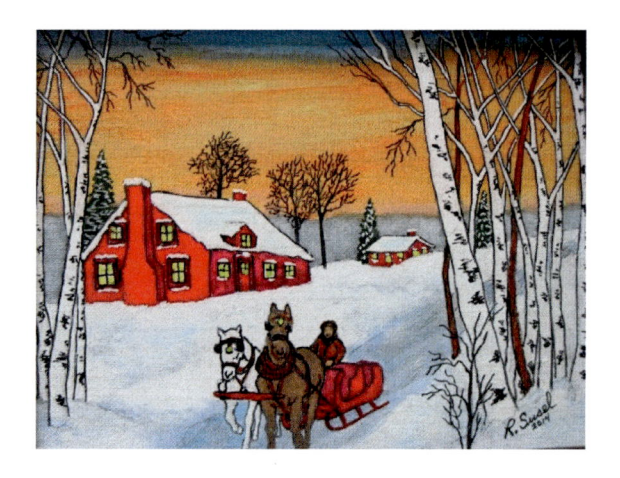

3. The Festive Season

My extended visit encompassed the "Festive Season - Saison des Fêtes" of Christmas and New Years. I experienced many of the well kept traditions, the warmth, the camaraderie and joy of the holidays. I am truly indebted to and continue to express my sincere gratitude to GrandPere Anctil and his wife Marie-Rose for their companionship, hospitality and cordiality.

On one of our trips Yvette, Armand's wife introduced her daughter Louise to me,
Armand is the one who makes his own booze a good man to know some agree.
Louise is the youngest and has two older sisters, Angelique and Josephine,
Louise works with dried flowers and creates arrangements of beauty unforeseen.
She operates a flower shop "Le Ruban Bleu" displaying bouquets for all to see,
Whenever GrandPere was busy I was told that I would be a welcome invitee.

Madame Yvette was well known for her famous tourtiere meat pie,
Her husband Armand and his Caribou for notoriety would also qualify.
Yvette and Louise introduced me to some specialities of their cuisine,

I learned pâté may be baked as pie or loaf or in a mold as pâté en terrine.
We had foie gras pâté (duck liver) and slightly chewy garlicky (snails) Escargot,
And cuisses de grenouille was not chicken but frogs legs really good and beaux.

We had delicious fruits de mer (seafood), les palourdes, (clams) and (cod) la morue,
Steamed Mussels (Moules à la vapeur) and Bouillabaisse made their debut.
Moules Marinières (mussels) with bread dipped into the garlicky, briny broth.
And halibut (le flétan) in a tomato-herb sauce which I dribbled on the tablecloth.
We also had oreilles de Christ (Christ ears) which are pieces of pork rind,
Fried until fat is all rendered and the rind is crispy, a blessing to mankind.

I visited often for the food I really enjoyed but treasured their company even more,
Their lively spirit (esprit) and joie de vivre (joy of life) as expressed I adore.
I also met Gaspard, the pig farmer and his wife Manon who makes charcuterie,
Saucisses (sausages), egg-like shaped poached quenelles, made with much esprit.
And many roulades (vegetable filled thinly rolled veal) called a Paupiette,
Pâtés, terrines, and galantines of veal coated with aspic I won't forget.

Jambon au sirop d'érable (ham with maple syrup) and rôti de porc (roast pork),
Ragoût de boulettes (meatball stew) and another bottle of wine to uncork.
Accompanied by baguette de pain, (French baguette) a long thin loaf with a crispy crust,
Baked directly on the hearth of the outdoor oven makes the meal fulfilling and robust.
The traditional country-style French bread, made the old-fashioned way,
Results in a lovely full-flavored loaf with a wonderful taste that will make your day

And delicacies, cretons (pork paté), boudin rouge (blood sausage), tourtière (pork pie),
Gras de porc (fat pork) and tête de cochon fromagée (head cheese), hunger to satisfy.
While jarrets de porc, (pork hocks) cooked in beer, or served gelled is customary,

They are exceptional served with French bread, and are in fact extraordinary.
Many delicacies were being prepared for the festive occasions coming up soon,
The heightened nostalgic activity in town from which no one was immune.

On one of our many trips GrandPere introduced me to Jean-Marc, the notary (notaire),
Who did testaments, contracts and who enjoyed a reputation of being honest and fair.
He had organized a private social club (members only) to run the village game night,
Permitting members to play cards, games of chance and bingo within the law alright.
Beside card games they played 75 ball bingo and raffled away turkeys,
Enjoyed many social and community events and warm spirited soirees.

Jean-Marc sat attentively on his platform at a desk with microphone in his left hand,
A buzzing machine had just released a yellow plastic winning ball on the stand.
Hr called out the number in a monotone voice "O soixante-sept; (O sixty-seven),"
He then put the ball in a socket on a console on his desk which was covered in vellum.
The players were concentrating being very attentive to follow his every call,
Methodically marking their bingo card papers with a distinctive scrawl.

Bingo was very popular in the past and for older folk it still was so endowed,
But as these people died off they were not being replaced by a younger crowd.
Bingo halls were full of people when smoking was permitted it formed a cloud,
A lot of smokers were chased away by the government when smoking was disallowed.
Women seeking company with friends liked the highly popular bingo soirees,
The golden age of bingo in the province was in the '60s and '70s across all diocese.

Huge Bingo games were played in stadiums and in church basements,
Prizes included cars, vacations and lots of cash at the many events.
Jean-Marc called out the next number, "N trente-cinq; (N thirty-five)",
Genevieve, the barber Giles wife, divided her attention between the calls, fully alive.
And the gossip of her two friends at the table talked nostalgically about the past,
When they played for food baskets, cheese, jams, potatoes, groceries so vast.

Bingo is strictly regulated by the government today and no alcohol is served,
Hurt most are the non-profit churches and community groups it was observed.
For a bingo operating licence in the province only non-profits can qualify,
Which only the Régie des alcools des courses et des jeux can supply.
Loto-Quebec is the province's gaming authority and by whom Bingo is guided,
The law even states a formula as to how monthly profits are to be divided.

The law states that once a player has a winning card, he must declare it out loud,
Otherwise he is not entitled to the prize and it can't be to them endowed.
In 1892, except for horse racing, gambling was prohibited by the criminal code,
In 1900, the right to hold bingo and raffles for charitable purposes was bestowed.
In 1925, rights were granted, gambling events at fairs and exhibitions could begin,
Irish Sweepstakes were popular, in 1950 gambling was no longer perceived as a sin.

Viewed as corruption by organized crime, war on illegal gambling was declared,
Even priests organizing bingo games for their parishes were threatened and scared.
In 1969, the Canadian government saw huge financial value in lotteries.
In 1970, provincial governments were authorized as lottery beneficiaries.
On March 14, 1970, Quebecers participated in the first Loto-Québec draw,
Licensed charitable and religious organizations held raffles the law oversaw.

Raffles with total prize value over $1,000 must be reported 30 days prior to the event,
60 days after a raffle an accounting statement to the licensing board must be sent.
Number of tickets printed, proceeds, prizes, expenses and cost as a record,
Winner names and addresses of prizes of $100 or more are reported to the board.
The law even specifies what the raffle ticket and stub must clearly include,
So that the buyer or player is informed and information is not misconstrued.

Gaspard's son, Gilles back from his trips stopped to have a spruce beer,
Recalled an occurrence and a story which he loudly proclaimed for all to hear.
Gilles is the one that delivers Armand's prized organic homemade booze,
And can interestingly talk and talk until everyone is in a peaceful snooze.
His charming manner drew people to him, he always had many tales to tell,
He had a special one for the many bingo players that went over well.

He said, in Montreal a man on the street was dying, he was hit by a bus,
A crowd of spectators gathered around to see what was all the fuss.
The dying man asked for a priest. "Somebody get me a priest!"
A policeman checked the crowd; no priest, or minister at least.
The dying man pleaded and asked for a priest once again,
From the crowd came a cane wielding eighty year old man then.

He told the cop, "I'm not a priest nor a Catholic, but I appear,
Since I live behind the Catholic Church over there for over fifty year,
And every night I have carefully listened to the Catholic litany,
Maybe I can give this dying man some comfort and sympathy".
The cop let the old gent kneel down beside the dying man,
The old guy shouted B-5. I-18. N-39. G-55. O-73 as loud as he can.

Gilles was a born raconteur with a knack for storytelling,
All kinds of magnificent and imaginary tales we found compelling.
He could keep people listening to him for hours on end,
Keeping us on the edge of our seats his art of narration would extend.
He notoriously told tall tales but never to cause deceit,
But out of kindness and love to entertain and never to mistreat.

His charming comical personality brought each story to life I confess,
When he entered the room saying, " wow, y'a du monde à messe!"
When he was interrupted and did not know what others were talking about,
  Ca mange quoi en hiver ça?" he was prone to loudly shout.
When someone attempted to embellish his story in some way,
"Mets-en, c'est pas de l'onguent!", he encouragingly would say.

He spoke of a farmer in a nearby town who went to see a movie,
With pet chicken on his shoulder he was denied entrance despite his plea.
No animals allowed in the theatre he went around the corner of the place,
Stuffing his pet chicken down his pants he entered with a straight face.
He made his way beside two nuns who also were nurses, he sat down firm,
The movie started as his pet chicken in his pants began to squirm.

For his pet the chicken in order to watch the movie he unzipped his pants,
One of the nuns became perturbed and incredibly gave him a glance.
She said to her friend, "I think this guy beside me is a pervert,
Because he has his thingie out, I think we should be on alert."
Her friend said, "Relax at our age and line of work we have seen them all,
Nothing to fear or need to raise an alarm, there is no one to call."

"Yes, you are probably right but just so you know, just to inform,
His little thingie is moving and eating my popcorn!"
The crowd heartedly laughed, they were thoroughly amused,
Which added more energy and Gilles was greatly enthused.
He continued talking about sister Mary another nurse and also a nun,
She had visited sick patients and ran out of gas like could happen to anyone.

Several blocks from a gas pump the only container she had was a bedpan,
She used it to get gas and having returned, transfer it into the car she began.
A group of people gathered and watched as she poured the last,
A driver poked his head out of his car window as he passed.
And said, "I swear if that car starts I'll pay for a special mass,
And thank the Lord you found a substitute for high priced gas.

GrandPere laughed a lot, some stories brought tears to his eyes,
Especially those involving the elderly with whom he could sympathize.
Gilles spoke about a widower meeting a widow at a social meal,
They met and enjoyed the companionship genuinely for real.
He gathered up his courage and timidly asked her to marry him,
After about 5 seconds of careful consideration, "Yes" she said with a grin.

After the meal, a few more pleasant exchanges they go their separate ways,
Next morning he couldn't remember was it no or yes his mind was ablaze.
He had her telephone number so he called gaining courage he explained,
He didn't remember as well as he used to and asked if her interest had vaned.
He reviewed the lovely evening and asked if she had said yes or no?
He was delighted to hear her say, "Yes, yes I will, my Romeo."

Then she continued, "I'm so truly glad that you called.
Because I couldn't remember who had asked me", she bawled.
Gilles continued entertaining as usual into the evening late,
He continued the great oral traditions and heritage to emulate.
Storytelling was a manner of chronicling events in communities,
And sharing and celebrating many of life's ambiguities.

Game night also has seen the game Jeu du Toc (Tock) being played,
A board game that the early settlers of Quebec had conveyed.
I watched and noticed it didn't seem to take too much thought to play,
Not really understanding the game, I tried to capture the rules anyway.
I present them here based on my observations as I best surveyed,
Should you try it you'll have to do so at your own risk I'm afraid.

TOC is played by 2 or 4 players, each using a different colour token. 4 tokens per player are placed in the player's "zone" on the board. The number 1 square is the player's starting square. The first player to move his 4 tokens around the board and reach his "home" (before his own square number 1 is the winner. You can enter "home" with any count high enough to reach "home", any exceeding unused count is discarded.

TOC is played with 52 playing cards (jokers removed). To begin 5 cards are dealt to each player on the first turn, then 4 cards on each of the 2 following turns. Players play in turn in a clockwise order. Aces and Kings are starter cards allowing a player to move a token to the start square (number 1). If a player does not have a starter card, he cannot advance a token and must discard a card.

Illustration of a traditional 2 or 4 player TOC board

If at any time a token lands on a square occupied by another token then it replaces it, and that token is placed back into the originating player's "zone" area. It may happen that a player replaces his own token.

No players can pass a token, either forward or backwards, that is on its starting (number 1) square. A token on its starting square (number 1) blocks all other tokens, in both directions (advancing or retreating) of the game. A token cannot pass a token of its own colour. You can pass other tokens without effect except with the king who eats everything in its path. The eaten tokens go back to the original players "zone" and need to be started again.

A player must play his cards even if it is to his disadvantage. Tokens are moved according to the value of the played card.

Ace — Make a move of 1 square, *or* use as a starter.

Jack — Make a move of 11 squares.
Queen — Make a move of 12 squares.
King — Make a move of 13 squares, *or* use as a starter. When a King moves 13 squares, it eats all tokens in its path, which then return to their respective "zones".
4 — Make a move of four squares backward.
7 — Make 7 individual moves of one square. The moves can be freely distributed among all of one's tokens.
Jack — Make a move of 11 squares *or* may swap one of his own tokens with any other token (opponent's or his own). Swapping two of his own tokens is equivalent to a pass.

All other cards allow you to move forward according to their own value.

Preparation for the birth of Our Savior Jesus Christ is the Advent,
It is the beginning of the liturgical calendar, as everyone will consent.
Some people bind evergreens to a circle of wire making Advent wreaths,
It holds four candles equally spaced a message each bequeaths.
Each Sunday of Advent a candle is lit the light of God coming onto the earth,
Marking the passage of time awaiting our saviour, Jesus Christ's birth.

Each candle symbolizes a Christian concept; hope for the first week,
peace (week two) joy (week three) and love (week four) that we all seek.
Three candles are violet the historic liturgical color while the forth is rose,
Rose is the liturgical color to rejoice on the third sunday of advent it bestows.
Candle lighting are accompanied with hymns and solemn prayers
A fifth white candle is often lit on Christmas Eve, Christ's arrival it declares.

Monique, the hair dresser went to Maxine's, the couturier for a new dress,
The one being displayed in the window she very much wanted to possess.
So she asked Maxine, 'May I try on that dress in the window, please?'
The question caught Maxine off guard causing her some unease,
She replied "Certainly not, Monique, use the fitting room she exclaimed,
Like everyone else instead of in the window you would be shamed!

Maxine could not believe that she had said such a thing,
She assured Monique that she had not meant it as a sting.

They both laughed at the suggestion of having a window tease,
And agreed that it depended on the watchers that it would please.
What if it was the Curée who would announce it to the entire diocese,
It may be good for business but they were unsure of any guarantees.

The Christmas season begins on the first Sunday of Advent,
Four Sundays before Christmas until Epiphany it is meant.
The festive season (saison des fêtes) lasts a full twelve days,
Every Christian religious family prayerfully and joyfully obeys.
Devout families participate in the Advent masses before the big day,
Erect nativity scenes and have a Christmas tree on display.

Gaspard had a terrible day fishing with no catch at all, so he made a stop,
On his way home, at Etienne's the poissonnier (the fishmonger) shop.
He ordered four large trout asking for them not to be cleaned at all,
So that he could tell his wife, that he caught them near the waterfall.
Etienne suggested and really insisted he take the salmon instead,
Explaining that Gaspard's wife, Manon had come in earlier not to be mislead.

Manon had said that if Gaspard came by, salmon I should tell you to take,
That's what she'd like for supper tonight, that's what she would like to make.
Gaspard stood in disbelief that now his wife knew he couldn't catch fish,
Etienne and Gaspard both had a good laugh that Manon would get her wish.
Etienne even cleaned the salmon before he wrapped it with a grin,
And Gaspard foiled in his deception shook his head much to his chagrin.

Christmas traditions of the people in my village focus on Christmas Eve,
People sleep during the day to be ready to feast and frolic they believe.
During the Christmas season church bells peel often and left longer to chime,
People follow traditions, church attendance increases and choirs grow with time.
It was not unusual to see a crowd of people squeezed into the paternal home,
To join in the family Christmas merry-making, never to spend Christmas alone.

People share folklore of Santa Claus (Pere Noel), and the lutins his helper elves.

Along with Mrs. Claus, (Mère Noël), Rudolph (Nez-Rouge) to fill the shelves.
They also have a lovely young woman la fée des étoiles (the Star Fairy),
Wielding a star-tipped wand clad in white-and-blue acting as emissary.
December 13 (winter solstice) is the shortest day, longest night of the year,
It's the feast of Sainte-Lucie that inspired the Star Fairy to appear.

Filbert the clock repairer came calling on the carpenter, Baptiste,
The carpenter's son Raymond informed him that he had just missed.
'Is there anything I can help you with?' Raymond politely asked,
"I know where all the tools are, if you want to borrow one" he gasped.
Or maybe I could take a message for my father for when he comes back,
"Well, it's difficult, Filbert says, wanting to talk to his father, walking to the shack.

"It's about my daughter, Marie who your brother Yvon got pregnant,
And that is why I feel that I must talk with your father as a parent."
Raymond thoughtfully replied, "You have to talk to Papa for sure,
I know that Papa charges $500 for the bull and $50 for the hog to procure,
But I don't know how much he gets for my brother Yvon for a fee,
Except that as always he never assures success nor makes any guarantee.

In advance of the carolers, came the children shouting, "The carolers are coming!",
This all happened despite the freezing rain, snow or cold that was numbing.
People going guignolée singing chants de noel (Christmas carols) door to door,
Collecting food and money for the benefit of the poor, they would implore.
Each home had prepared a table with gift and for those who wished to have a drink,
They were offered shots of warm apple cider or whisky blanc to warm them up I think.

The carolers, sang in front of the door until invited to enter by the homeowner,
They refreshed themselves, received the gifts and left; going on to the next donor..
A sleigh or truck followed the group into which were emptied the gifts and donations,

They were then distributed to the highly respected helping the poor organizations.
Bolstered by drink their singing grew louder and more boisterous their dissertations,
Progressing along they were escorted by children and all the dogs of those locations.

The guignolée tradition was practiced throughout December and into New Year's Eve,
At each house, they warmed their feet and throat, a snack and a gift they did receive.
A pork loin was the most prized gift they were hoping for that awaited them at the door,
Which people put aside specially for this purpose during the holiday butcher's chore.
Taking part in the guignole was a form of rejoicing with song, laughter well expressed,
Well known, La guignolée *song* was heard everywhere on the occasion of this quest.

CHANSON DE LA GUIGNOLÉE	(English Translation)
Bonjour le maître et la maîtresse	Hello Master and Mistress
Et tous les gens de la maison,	And all the people in the house
Nous avons fait une promesse	We have made a promise
De v'nir vous voir une fois l'an.	To come and see you
Une fois l'an ce n'est pas grand-chose	Once a year it's not a big deal
Qu'un petit morceau de chignée,	Just a small contribution
Si vous voulez.	If you want to
Si vous voulez rien nous donner,	If you want to give us nothing
Dites nous lé.	Tell us that
Nous prendrons la fille aînée,	We will take the eldest daughter
Nous y ferons chauffer les pieds!	We will make her feet warm
La Ignolée! La Ignoloche!	The Ignolée! The Ignoloche!
Pour mettre du lard dans ma poche	To put the lard into my pocket
Nous ne demandons pas grand-chose	We are not asking for very much
Pour l'arrivée.	To come up with
Vingt-cinq ou trente pieds de chignée,	Twenty five or thirty feet of contribution
Si vous voulez.	If you want to
Nous sommes cinq ou six bons drôles,	We are five or six funny guys
Et si notre chant n'vous plaît pas	And if our chant does not please you
Nous ferons du feu dans les bois	We will set fire in the woods
Étant à l'ombre,	Being in the shade
On entendra chanter l'coucou	We will hear the cuckoo
Et la Coulombe!	And the coulomb

Rue Principal was decked out with an impressive brilliant array of light,
A tall decorated Christmas tree in the main square was a festive sight.
At the Centre d'Accueil area artisans organized Marche de Noel (Christmas market),
So that buying a treasured gift for someone a person wouldn't forget.
The warmly decorated centre d'Accueil was a world of colour and was very bright,
The market showcased products that made you crave more, wetting your appetite.

Louise displayed topiary plants, holly, myrtle, bay laurel an aromatic evergreen,
Shaped wire cages with small-leaved ivy, to be admired most beautiful ever seen.
Works of art, floral displays, beautiful thick quilts, slippers and colourful aprons,
Even a small bar serving ice cold beer, cider and wine to very thirsty patrons.
There was our herbalist Clémence, dispensing advice along with his tea,
Surrounded by people listening to his cure all remedies sold without guarantee.

A farmer found a visitor to the market had driven his car into a ditch,
Helping him, his big strong horse named Bisou to the car he hitched.
And yelled real loud, "Pull, Champion, pull." But Bisou didn't move.
Then the farmer hollered, "Pull, Calisson, pull." Bisou didn't improve.
Then the farmer nonchalantly and softly said, "Pull, Bisou, pull."
And the horse very easily dragged the car out of the ditch in full.

The motorist asked the farmer although he was appreciative and full of praise,
Why had he called his horse by the wrong name two times and was amazed.
The farmer told him that old Bisou was very strong but he was blind,
He was a good work horse and very helpful he always was so inclined.
Always trained to listen very well and respectfully to comply
But if he thought he was the only one pulling, he wouldn't even try!

The market had hand-knitted woolens, wood carvings, hand-crafted toys and doll beds,

Bits of wool and pieces of cloth, needles, pins, buttons, scissors, cushions and threads.
There was jewelry, blankets, clothing, sculptures, warm mittens and big colourful bowls,
Jams and syrups, maple syrup, maple butter, maple sugar, pastries, bread and rolls.
Spicy apple juice, terrines, mousses, sausages, smoked venison and marinades,
Enthusiastic excitement, fiddle music, gigue dancing, joie de vivre (joy of life) pervades.

There were hand-knitted woolens, hand-crafted toys, ceramics, paintings, wines,
Boutiques with jewelry, pottery, clothing, floral arrangements and lots of signs.
Beautiful wreaths, sculptures, baked goods, hats and gloves and fancy sweets,
Maple syrup, maple butter, maple sugar candy, and liqueurs among the treats.
Even a small café for coffee and tasty snacks and even a crepe stand,
Crepes as fast food at its best with a range of fillings to meet demand.

Some bought fancy expensive liqueurs, spirits and imported French wines,
Others had homemade wines from potatoes, cherries, rhubarb or combined.
Still others preferred to indulge in Caribou bought their booze from Armand,
Served, these drinks were a sign of hospitality and conviviality voila.
Families gathered and spent time together, they went to Midnight Mass,
Fortified with spirits they helped the choir with singing no one could surpass.

Alphonse, the inventor, had a perfect scheme to make some cash,
His plan was to hold a raffle and raise lots of money in a flash.
For ($100.00) cent piastres Alphonse bought a donkey to prove his concept,
To pick up the donkey the next day, he looked forward to the prospect.
When Alphonse came for it he was told the donkey had died.
So Alphonse asked for his money back but the farmer replied.

That he had given the money to his wife and that it had been spent,
So Alphonse loaded the dead donkey and took it in any event.
The farmer asked him, 'With the dead donkey, what was he gonna do?

Alphonse said "I'll raffle him off as planned, a lottery I will pursue.
The farmer objected saying you can't raffle off a donkey who is dead,
But Alphonse smiling said, "Just don't let the dead donkey news spread".

A month later the farmer asked Alphonse about his dead donkey scam,
Alphonse said, 'I raffled him off. I sold 500 tickets at $2.00 each as was my plan.
Sticking his chest out he proudly said a huge profit of $698.00 I have attained,
The amazed farmer was curious and asked if anyone complained,
The only one who found out was the raffle winner, but it was explained,
The inquisitive farmer wanted to know how peace had been maintained.

When he came to claim his prize I gave him his $2.00 back plus $200.00 more,
Which is double the going value of a donkey, so he thought it was a great score.
Alphonse said that he tried to talk the Curée into using it to raise needed funds,
Telling him about his proof of concept but the entire scheme the Curée shuns.
He say first I have no right to hold a raffle it's against the government legislation,
If I do this he said he would have to report me to save his own reputation.

Le sapin de Noël or l'arbre de noël refers to the Christmas tree,
Put in people's homes beginning in December with great esprit.
Usually with frenzied activity, by the children it was decorated,
With little adult help, the huge tree in the house was populated.
Along with the tree, people have a crèche (the nativity scene),
Complete manger, hay, a star and with a hand crafted figurine.

The Nativity scene beautifully on display often got the Curée's blessing,
Below are the words while visiting as part of his greetings he would bring.
"Lord, bless all who look upon this manger; for our dear saviour,
May it remind us of the humble birth of Jesus, this our behaviour.
And raise our thoughts to him, who is God-with-us and Savior of all,
Who lives and reigns forever and ever. Amen"; his words echoed in the hall.

The Curée came, it was obvious someone was home at the house he was calling,
But no answer came to his repeated knocks at the door, which was appalling.
So he left a business card printed "Revelation 3:20" on the back in the door,
In the Sunday offering his card was returned with "Genesis 3:10" he could not ignore.
Revelation 3:20 begins "Behold, I stand at the door and knock". very sacred,
Genesis 3:10 was, "I heard your voice in the garden and I was afraid for I was naked."

Guests and neighbors arrived cheerfully many with their children in tow,
They removed their mittens, coats, boots, scarves, tuques and chapeaux.
Pretty soon the children go upstairs to sleep, five or six to a bed they overflow,
The older children will accompany the adults to mass through the snow.
Grandma usually stayed home watching the children making no noise and was steady,
Making sure that when everyone returned home all would be deliciously ready.

In the meantime Grandma was in the kitchen attending to cooking her stew,
For the invitees who take a little shot GrandPere took out his caribou.
She got some help as the table was set with the utmost of loving care,
The hand-embroidered tablecloth set off the white china and silverware.
A mixture of bottles of red and white wines, amid the candles, were placed,
With white whisky, blueberry wine, large and small glasses were evenly spaced.

Some drove their cars, others walked and still others came by sleigh,
Bundled up in blankets, to midnight mass they hurried without delay.
In church Christmas day is only the beginning of the celebration,
Singing "Gloria in excelsis Deo" (Glory to God in the Highest) in adoration.
We continued to sing this beautiful song until January 6 the day of Epiphany,
That is also the day that most people take down their decorated Christmas tree.

Before midnight mass, ceremoniously carried into church was a cradle,

At midnight, a wax Jesus was placed in it among the hay from the stable.
The celebration began in church, where the Nativity crèche was on display,
A statue of the Infant Jesus was brought in procession, his birth to convey.
Placed at midnight alongside Mary and Joseph, donkey, and an ox in the hay,
Gloria in excelsis Deo (Glory to God) was sung ending the gospel that we pray.

Latin text (Version in use)	English translation
Glória in excélsis Deo	Glory to God, to the highest heaven
And in terra pax homínibus bonae voluntátis.	and on earth peace to men of good .
Laudámus te,	We praise you,
Benedícimus te,	We bless you,
Adorámus te,	We adore you,
Glorificámus te,	We glorify you,
Grátias ágimus tibi propter magnam glóriam tuam,	We thank you for your immense glory.
Dómine Deus, Rex cæléstis,	Lord God, King of Heaven,
Deus Pater omnipotens.	God the Father Almighty.
Dómine Fili Unigénite, Iesu Christe,	Lord, only Son Jesus Christ,
Dómine Deus, Agnus Dei, Fílius Patris,	Lord God, Lamb of God, the Son of the Father,
Which tollis peccáta mundi, miserére nobis;	You who take away the sin of the world, have mercy on us.
Which tollis peccáta mundi	You who take away the sin of the world,
Súscipe deprecatiónem nostram,	Receive our prayer.
Who sedes ad dexteram Patris,	You who sit at the right hand of the Father,
Miserere nobis.	Have mercy on us.
Quóniam tu solus Sanctus,	For You alone are holy,
You solus Dóminus,	You alone are Lord,
You solus Altíssimus,	You alone are the Most High,
Iesu Christe,	Jesus Christ,
Cum Sancto Spíritu,	With the Holy Spirit,
In glória Dei Patris.	In the glory of God the Father.
Amen.	Amen.

The procession of the Christ Child was an essential element of the tradition,

Making a visit to the crèche surrounding this celebration was a desired mission.
On Christmas day mass is celebrated three times with chiming bells,
The nativity Midnight Mass also called "Angels' Mass" welcoming the faithful it compels.
The second service is the "Shepherds' Mass" or Dawn Mass following the first,
The third, Christmas Day Mass called "Mass of the Divine Word" is well rehearsed.

Custom has it that once midnight mass or the dawn mass is prayed,
A visit to the crèche by the whole family to see the Infant Jesus is made.
They come to see the baby Jesus lying in a manger and to give their affection,
And leave their offering to the Infant Jesus with the beautiful angel collection.
Attendance at one or more masses on Christmas Eve would not be complete,
Without a visit to the crèche (manger), the Infant Jesus to worship and meet.

Church crèches with Nativity figures appeared back in 1640, when erected,
By the Ursuline nuns, a religious order from France who also perfected.
The bee's wax figurines of the Christ Child, angels and animals, all done by hand,
They guarded their secret, while churches adopted the practice throughout the land.
That is how re-enacting the crèche in which baby Jesus was born began,
From the start of the colony the manger continues to be replicated by man.

We are reminded of what guided the three wise men, the scene includes a star,
Representing the one that led to the manger of Caspar, Melchior and Balthazar.
Bringing the whole family gliding over the powdery snow, was quite a sight,
In the middle of the night we celebrated the passage from darkness to light.
Isaiah and the Gospel of Luke announce the birth of Jesus as the "Prince of Peace",
That message of the angels to the shepherds is the season's centerpiece.

As part of his homily, the Curée spoke about Christmas traditions with precision,

He explained that Christmas trees were secular having nothing to do with religion.
He warned about extravagance, people decorating so as not to be outdone,
Saying there was no right date to put up or to take down the tree, it is for fun.
And people don't have to put up a tree at all. His advice was to do what works for you.
He assured everyone that they were beloved children of God through and through.

Christmas carols "Chants de Noel" or hymns were sung by the marvelous choir,
People listened attentively to the choral arrangements as they transpired.
Below are several to capture and illustrate the most beautiful words on earth,
Sung in adoration and a crescendo in memory of our saviour's birth.

IL EST NÉ LE DIVIN ENFANT - He is born, the Heavenly Child

French Lyrics	English Translation
Chorus: Il est né le divin enfant,	Chorus: He is born, the Heav'nly Child,
Jouez hautbois, résonnez musettes	Oboes play; set bagpipes sounding
Il est né le divin enfant,	He is born, the Heav'nly Child.
Chantons tous son avènement	Let all sing His nativity.
Depuis plus de quatre mille ans,	'Tis four thousand years and more,
Nous le promettaient les prophètes	Prophets have foretold His coming,
Depuis plus de quatre mille ans,	'Tis four thousand years and more,
Nous attendions cet heureux temps.	Have we waited this happy hour.
Chorus	Chorus
Ah ! Qu'il est beau, qu'il est charmant	Ah, how lovely, Ah, how fair,
Ah ! que ses grâces sont parfaites	What perfection is His graces,
Ah ! Qu'il est beau, qu'il est charmant	Ah, how lovely, Ah, how fair.
Qu'il est doux ce divin enfant.	Child divine, so gentle there.
Chorus	Chorus

Une étable est son logement	In a stable lodged is He,
Un peu de paille est sa couchette,	Straw is all He has for cradle.
Une étable est son logement	In a stable lodged is He,
Pour un dieu quel abaissement.	Oh how great humility!

Chorus / Chorus

Partez, grands rois de l'Orient	Leave great king of the orient
Venez vous unir à nos fêtes	Come to our holiday
Partez, grands rois de l'Orient	Leave great king of the orient
Venez adorer cet enfant.	Come adore this child

Chorus / Chorus

Il veut nos cœurs, il les attend	He wants our hearts, He's waiting for them
Il est là pour faire leur conquête	He is there to conquer them
Il veut nos cœurs, il les attend	He wants our hearts, He's waiting for them
Donnons-les lui donc promptement.	Let us give him them promptly

Chorus / Chorus

O Jésus! O Roi tout-puissant	Jesus Lord, O King with power,
Tout petit enfant que vous êtes,	A little babe that you are,
O Jésus! O Roi tout-puissant,	Jesus Lord, O King with power,
Régnez sur nous entièrement.	Rule o'er us from this glad hour.

Chorus / Chorus

MINUIT CHRÉTIEN - Midnight, Christians

This beautiful Christmas carol is traditionally sung at midnight mass.

French Lyrics	English Translation
Minuit, chrétiens, c'est l'heure solennelle	Midnight, Christians, it is the solemn hour
Où l'Homme-Dieu descendit jusqu'à nous,	When God as man descended among us
Pour effacer la tache originelle,	To expunge the stain of original sin
Et de son Père arrêter le courroux.	And to put an end to the wrath of his father.
Le monde entier tressaille d'espérance,	The entire world thrills with hope
À cette nuit qui lui donne un Sauveur.	On this night which gives us a savior.
Peuple, à genoux, attends ta délivrance	People, on your knees, *attend** your deliverance.
Noël! Noël! Voici le Rédempteur!	

Noël! Noël! Voici le Rédempteur!	Christmas! Christmas! Here is the Redeemer! Christmas! Christmas! Here is the Redeemer!
De notre foi que la lumière ardente Nous guide tous au berceau de l'Enfant, Comme autrefois une étoile brillante Y conduisit les chefs de l'Orient. Le Roi des rois naît dans une humble crèche; Puissants du jour, fiers de votre grandeur, À votre orgueil, c'est de là que Dieu prêche. Courbez vos fronts devant le Rédempteur! Courbez vos fronts devant le Rédempteur!	The ardent light of our Faith, Guides us all to the cradle of the infant, As in ancient times a brilliant star Conducted the Magi there from the orient. The King of kings was born in a humble manger; O mighty ones of today, proud of your grandeur, It is to your pride that God preaches. Bow your heads before the Redeemer! Bow your heads before the Redeemer!
Le Rédempteur a brisé toute entrave, La Terre est libre et le Ciel est ouvert. Il voit un frère où n'était qu'un esclave, L'amour unit ceux qu'enchaînait le fer. Qui lui dira notre reconnaissance? C'est pour nous tous qu'il naît, qu'il souffre et meurt. Peuple, debout! Chante ta délivrance. Noël! Noël! Chantons le Rédempteur! Noël! Noël! Chantons le Rédempteur!	The Redeemer has broken all shackles. The earth is free and heaven is open. He sees a brother were there was once but a slave; Love unites those who restrain the sword. Who will tell him our gratitude? It is for us all that he was born, that he suffered and died. People, stand up, sing your deliverance! Christmas! Christmas! Let us sing the Redeemer! Christmas! Christmas! Let us sing the Redeemer!

D'OÙ VIENS-TU, BERGÈRE? Where do you come from shepherd? Being asked by the soloist, the shepherd recalls the miracle in the stable.

French Lyrics	English Translation
Soloist: D'où viens-tu bergère? D'où viens-tu?	Where do you come from shepherd? Where do you come

Group: D'où viens-tu bergère? D'où viens-tu?	Where do you come from shepherd? Where do you come from
Je viens de l'étable, de m'y promener J'ai vu un miracle, ce soir arrivé.	I come from the stable, to walk there I saw a miracle tonight arrive
S: Qu'as-tu vu, bergère? Qu'as-tu vu? G: Qu'as-tu vu, bergère? Qu'as-tu vu? J'ai vu dans la crèche un petit enfant. Sur la paille fraîche, mis bien tendrement.	What did you see shepherd? What did you see? What did you see shepherd? What did you see? I saw in the manger a little child On fresh straw put tenderly
S: Rien de plus, bergère? Rien de plus? G: Rien de plus, bergère? Rien de plus? Y a trois petits anges descendus du ciel. Chantant les louanges du Père éternel.	Nothing more shepherd? Nothing more? Nothing more shepherd? Nothing more? There are three little angels descended from the sky Singing the praises of the eternal Father
S: Est-il beau, bergère? Es-t-il beau? G: Est-il beau, bergère? Es-t-il beau? Plus beau que la lune, aussi le soleil Jamais dans le monde, on vit son pareil.	Is he beautiful, shepherd? Is he beautiful? Is he beautiful, shepherd? Is he beautiful? More beautiful than the moon and the sun Never in the world do we see the same
S: Allons-y, bergère. Allons-y G: Allons-y, bergère. Allons-y Portons-lui des langes, aussi des drapeaux Et pour sa couchette, un petit berceau.	Let us go, shepherd Let us go, Let us go, shepherd Let us go, Let's bring him diapers, also flags And for its berth, a small cradle

Douce Nuit, Sainte Nuit - Silent Night, Holy Night
The well known English version is:

Silent Night, Holy Night
All is calm, All is bright
Round yon virgin Mother and child
Holy infant so tender and mild

Sleep in heavenly peace
Sleep in heavenly peace

French Lyrics	English Translation
Douce nuit, sainte nuit	Sweet night holy night
Dans les cieux L'astre luit.	In the heavens! The star shines.
Le mystère annoncé s'accomplit	The mystery announced is fulfilled
Cet enfant sur la paille endormi,	This child on the straw asleep,
C'est l'amour infini	It is infinite love!
C'est l'amour infini	It is infinite love!
Saint enfant, doux agneau	Holy child, sweet lamb
Qu'il est grand ! Qu'il est beau	How big it is! How handsome he is
Entendez résonner les pipeaux	Hear resonating the pipes
Des bergers conduisant leurs troupeaux	Shepherds leading their flocks
Vers son humble berceau	Towards his humble cradle!
Vers son humble berceau	Towards his humble cradle!
C'est vers nous qu'il accourt,	It is towards us that he rushes,
En un don sans retour	In a gift without return!
De ce monde ignorant de l'amour,	From this ignorant world of love,
Où commence aujourd'hui son séjour,	Where today begins his stay,
Qu'il soit Roi pour toujours	May he be King forever
Qu'il soit Roi pour toujours	May he be King forever
Quel accueil pour un Roi	What a welcome for a King
Point d'abri, point de toit	No shelter, no roof
Dans sa crèche il grelotte de froid	In his crib he shivered with cold
O pécheur, sans attendre la croix,	O sinner, without waiting for the cross,
Jésus souffre pour toi	Jesus suffers for you!
Jésus souffre pour toi	Jesus suffers for you!
Paix à tous ! Gloire au ciel	Peace to all! Glory to Heaven
Gloire au sein maternel,	Glory within motherhood,
Qui pour nous, en ce jour de Noël,	Who for us, on this Christmas day,
Enfanta le Sauveur éternel,	Child the eternal Savior,
Qu'attendait Israël	What was Israel waiting for?
Qu'attendait Israël	What was Israel waiting for?

As the religious celebration ends, people flow out into the cold outside,
The temperature has dropped further as everyone dreams of a fireside.
Homeward bound gliding over icy roads and slippery fields they return,
Some of them so cold that for frostbite they have urgent concerns.

After the family's visit to the crèche (nativity manger) and blessing from the priest,
They returned to the Christmas gathering to have the réveillon, a nightlong feast.

Finally they arrived in the door, shaking off their frost-covered overcoats,
Boots are removed and everyone settles in with a drink to sooth their throats.
They wish one another a warm Merry Christmas, chaleureux Joyeux Fete Noel,
The réveillon is a lavish and elaborate banquet where traditional dishes excel.
Le Réveillon takes place Christmas eve with families gathering together,
Attending midnight mass and returning to a feast, no matter the weather

Maple logs are blazing in the fireplace, warmth is spreading everywhere,
Everyone is relaxed and joyfully awaiting the utmost feast extraordinaire.
They were all welcomed to an abundance and variety of appetizing dishes,
Festive merriment, music and dancing as well as sincere hearty best wishes.
Everyone except the children were awake at the feast for most of the night,
The food and libations provided sustenance and satisfied the most demanding appetite.

This was the Réveillon and we joyfully took our places at the table admiring the spread,
We began with country-style thick pea soup and some home baked crusty bread.
The soup enriched with pork and flavoured with chopped parsley and sage,
A spoon could almost stand up in it by itself; and in small talk we engage.

There was butter, ham, turkey with all the trimmings relishes and gravy,
Ragoût de patte (pig's feet stew), pâtés, tourtiere, tasty morsels of miscellany.

Next came cipaille, a thick pie filled with various layers (rabbit, chicken, duck) of meat,
With layers of onions and pastry, seasoned with herbs, covered with pastry complete.
Then came the golden stuffed turkey, surrounded by red cabbage steamed,
With a warm blueberry sauce, baked beans, buttery mashed potatoes creamed.
White beans cooked with fried onion, molasses a few morsels of salt pork,
Washed down with smooth, sparkly, wine with more bottles left to uncork.

And of course there was the traditional tourtière (Meat pie) and pig's feet stew,
The turkey had apple, raisin and brandy stuffing washed down with home-brew.
There were many other delicious preparations, dishes and vegetables too,
We cleaned our plates emptied our glasses trying not to leave any residue.
We had la bûche de noel (yule log), doughnuts cooked in boiling syrup hit the spot,
Tarte au sucre and tarte à la farlouche, (cream and sugar Pie), steaming hot.

Also many variants of quiche, such as quiche au fromage (quiche with cheese),

And quiche aux champignons (quiche with mushrooms) were sure to please.
Also scrumptious quiche florentine (spinach) and provençale (tomatoes),
With incredibly wonderful ingredients kept secret and couldn't be disclosed.
As a starter the pea soup was served topped with crisply fried bacon and fresh chives,
The smooth soup was flavourful, until the savoury and tasty Tourtiére tart arrived.

Buttered vegetables and some pickled in a delicious blend of festive spices,
Formed the perfect complement for the meat pie dispensed in triangular slices.
For dessert, a bûche de Noël (Yule log), a rolled sponge cake was served,
Chocolate iced and decorated, it's wooden log appearance is well deserved.
Tarte au sucre (sugar pie) and maple crème brûlée with a golden, shell,
Creamy and smooth little squares of delicious maple cream fudge, très belle.

Families without children exchanged gifts after Santa's appearance,
Some left gifts under the tree foregoing the Santa custom adherence.
Those with children always had Santa Claus delivering the gifts,
To be unwrapped in the morning, hopefully they were on their wish lists.
Children desperately tried to stay up with the adults, not to miss a thing,
Enjoying the music, and dreaming of opening presents that Santa would bring.

We waited for Santa Claus to come by for a visit with a huge bag of toys,
Some of the presents would be saved for New Year's Day for the girls and boys.

GrandPere had the worst timing being off on an errand not seeing the jolly elf,
Everyone present were sure that GrandPere had never seen Santa himself.
Quietly and unannounced the jolly elf snuck on tip toes in the door,
He worked attracting as little attention as possible but was hard to ignore.

Le Père Noël (Santa Clause) winked just like GrandPere but looked much fatter,
Had a hearty laugh, a white beard, wore a red suit and offered not much chatter.
He was in a gigantic rush, quickly emptying his big sack on the floor,
As the children soundly slept, the room took on the look of a toy store.
As quietly as he had come, he suddenly disappeared and was gone,
Knowing that the children were very well taken care of, awaiting dawn.

According to the Government Department of Fish and Game,
Each summer both male and female reindeer grow antlers the same.
In late November male reindeers drop their antlers and everything.
Female reindeer keep their antlers till after they give birth in the spring.
So every one of Santa's reindeer as pictured had to be a girl it seems
Dragging the jolly fat man all around the world fulfilling dreams.

The feast continued with cheerful entertainment and Christmas songs,
With translated lyrics or with only the melody being retained where it belongs.
Jingle Bells is a good example it becomes Vive le vent. Long Live the Wind,
Below are some Christmas songs that were sung at the auberge, (inn).

VIVE LE VENT - Long live the wind
Vive le vent replaces "Jingle Bells" in French.

French Lyrics	English Translation
Vive le vent, vive le vent, vive le vent d'hiver	Long live the wind, long live the wind,
qui s'en va sifflant, soufflant dans les grands sapins verts.	Long live the winter wind, Which goes whistling, blowing In the big green Christmas trees!
Vive le temps, vive le temps, vive le temps d'hiver	Long live the time, long live the time,
boules de neige et jour de l'an et bonne année grand-mère.	Long live the winter time, Snowballs and new year's day and happy new year Grandma
Sur le long chemin	

tout blanc de neige blanche un vieux monsieur s'avance avec sa canne dans la main et tout là-haut le vent qui siffle dans les branches puis souffle la romance qu'il chantait petit enfant	Along the long trail All white from the white snow An old man advances With his cane in his hand. And up at the top the wind blows Which whistles in the branches Blows on him the romance That he sang as a young child
Et le vieux monsieur descend vers le village C'est l'heure où tout est sage et l'ombre danse au coin du feu Mais dans chaque maison il flotte un air de fête partout la table est prête et l'on entend la même chanson	And the old man Goes down toward the village, It's the time when everyone is good And the shadow dances near the fire. But in each house There's a festive air Everywhere the table is ready And you hear the same song

Le petit renne au nez rouge   The Little Reindeer with the Red Nose
This song tells the story of 'Rudolph, the Red-Nosed Reindeer'.

French Lyrics	English Translation
Quand la neige recouvre la verte Finlande Et que les rennes traversent la lande Le vent dans la nuit Au troupeau parle encore de lui	When the snow covers the green Finland And that the reindeer cross the moor Wind in the night The herd still talks about him
On l'appelait Nez Rouge Ah comme il était mignon Le p'tit renne au nez rouge Rouge comme un lumignon	It was called Red Nose Ah how cute it was The little red-nosed reindeer Red as a light
Son p'tit nez faisait rire Chacun s'en moquait beaucoup On allait jusqu'à dire Qu'il aimait boire un p'tit coup	His little nose was laughing Everyone made fun of them We went so far as to say That he liked to drink a little punch
Une fée qui l'entendit Pleurer dans le noir Pour le consoler, lui dit : "Viens au paradis ce soir"	A fairy who heard her Crying in the dark To console him, she said: "Come to paradise tonight"
Comme un ange Nez Rouge Tu conduiras dans le ciel Avec ton p'tit nez rouge	As an angel Red Nose You will drive in the sky With your little red nose

Le chariot du Père Noël	The chariot of Santa Claus
Quand ses frères le virent	When his brothers saw him
d'allure aussi leste	Also look good
Suivre très digne les routes célestes	Follow very heavenly routes
Devant ses ébats	In front of his frolics
Plus d'un renne resta baba	More than one reindeer remained baba
On l'appelait Nez Rouge	It was called Red Nose
Ah comme il était mignon	Ah how cute it was
Le p'tit renne au nez rouge	The little red-nosed reindeer
Rouge comme un lumignon	Red as a light
Maintenant qu'il entraîne	Now that it
Son char à travers les cieux	His chariot through the heavens
C'est lui le roi des rennes	He is the king of the reindeer
Et son nez fait des envieux	And his nose is envious
Vous fillettes et garçons	Girls and boys
Pour la grande nuit	For the big night
Si vous savez vos leçons	If you know your lessons
Dès que sonnera minuit	As soon as midnight
Ce petit point qui bouge	This small point that moves
Ainsi qu'une étoile au ciel	As well as a star in the sky
C'est le nez de Nez Rouge	It's the nose of Red Nose
Annonçant le Père Noël (x2)	Announcing Santa Claus (x2)

PETIT PAPA NOËL - Small Father Christmas
This sweet lullaby does not have an English equivalent, but it has lulled many children to sleep during the holidays.

French Lyrics	English Translation
C'est la belle nuit de Noël	It's a beautiful Christmas night
La neige étend son manteau blanc	Snow spreads its white coat
Et les yeux levés vers le ciel	And eyes lift toward the sky
À genoux, les petits enfants	On their knees, small children
Avant de fermer les paupières	Before closing their eyes
Font une dernière prière.	Say a last prayer.
Petit papa Noël	Little Santa Claus
Quand tu descendras du ciel	When you come down from the sky
Avec des jouets par milliers	With thousands of toys
N'oublie pas mon petit soulier.	Don't forget my little stocking.
Mais avant de partir	But before you leave

Il faudra bien te couvrir	You should dress well
Dehors tu vas avoir si froid	Outside you will be so cold
C'est un peu à cause de moi.	And it's kind of my fault.
Le marchand de sable est passé	The sandman has passed
Les enfants vont faire dodo	The children are going to sleep
Et tu vas pouvoir commencer	And you will be able to begin,
Avec ta hotte sur le dos	With your sack on your back,
Au son des cloches des églises	To the sound of church bells,
Ta distribution de surprises.	Your distribution of surprises.
Il me tarde que le jour se lève	I can't wait for sunrise
Pour voir si tu m'as apporté	To see if you brought me
Tous les beaux joujoux que je vois en rêve	All the lovely toys that I see in my dreams
Et que je t'ai commandés.	And that I had asked you for.

MON BEAU SAPIN (My beautiful pine)

The French version of 'Oh Christmas Tree', based on the German song 'O Tannenbaum'.

French Lyrics	English Translation
Mon beau sapin, roi des forêts	My beautiful pine, king of the forests
Que j'aime ta verdure	That i like your greenness
Quand par l'hiver, bois et guérets	When by the winter woods and fallow lands
Sont dépouillés de leurs attraits	Their attractions are totally stolen
Mon beau sapin, roi des forêts	My beautiful pine, king of forests
Tu gardes ta parure.	You keep your decoration
Toi que Noël planta chez nous	You that Christmas planted at our home
Au saint Anniversaire	The holly birthday
Joli sapin, comme ils sont doux,	Nice pine, like you are soft
Et tes bonbons, et tes joujoux	And your candies, and your toys
Toi que Noël planta chez nous	You that Christmas planted at our home
Tu répands la lumière.	You spread the light
Mon beau sapin, tes verts sommets	My beautiful pine, your green peaks
Et leur fidèle ombrage	And their loyal shadow
De la foi qui ne ment jamais	The faith that never lies
De la constance et de la paix.	The constancy and the peace
Mon beau sapin tes verts sommets	My beautiful pine, your green peaks
M'offrent la douce image.	The peaks offer the soft sensation.

Mon beau sapin, roi des forêts	My beautiful pine, king of the forests
Que j'aime ta parure	That i like your decoration
Et quand la neige blanchit tes traits	And when the snow whitens your lines
Que ta verdure disparaît	That your greenness disappear
Mon beau sapin, roi des forêts	My beautiful pine, king of the forests
Tu brilles dans l'Azur.	You shine in the Azur.

Interspersed with the songs was lively fiddle music and stories of yore,
Based on beliefs and passed by each generation by oral tradition, a real lore.
Legends always enlivened the evening particularly Christmas folk tales of old,
An old story of la chasse-galerie (The Bewitched Canoe) is often retold.

Back in the late 1800s, many men spent long winters in remote logging camps,
Without their loved ones they were lonely as reflected in their gigues and chants.
They worked there to support their families back in their villages and towns,
Transport being nonexistent, coming back for a short visit was out of bounds.
So they had to spend the whole season far from their homes and found it rough,
These lonely homesick men wanting to celebrate the réveillon found it tough.

So they made a deal with the Prince of Darkness that is the devil,
He would make their canoe fly over the forests, valley and hill.
So they could go back to their homes for the one Christmas night.
They all agreed on all three of the devil's conditions outright.
They had to be back at camp before 6 o'clock in the morning; they could not swear,
And they could not touch a church steeple with their canoe while in midair.

Breaking any one of those rules would damn their souls to hell forever,
Despite the risk, the homesick men agreed and off they flew, however.
The reunion with their beloved women were cheerful and joyous indeed,
They spent the night drinking whiskey-blanc and dancing fulfilling their need.

Realizing the late hour, they hurried back to the canoe so as not to impede,
Wanting desperately to return to camp before the devils deadline at full speed.

In their intoxicated state they were a lot more likely to swear,
Or to accidentally hit a church steeple by not being fully aware.
When one of them got agitated and almost swore, he was restrained,
Eventually though he broke free and swore while being so inflamed.
They then crashed into a tall tree and their doomed souls come into view,
As they fly forever across the sky, at Christmas in their bewitched canoe.

The fiddlers were known especially for their jigging or clogging manners,
Created while seated tapping both feet on the floor in rhythmic patterns.
It adds appreciable percussion as accompaniment to the composition,
Utilisaient les cuillères (playing spoons) greatly aided the rendition.
Striking spoons against each other or hands, legs and knees,
Creates a variety of sounds adding them to the routines in a breeze.

GrandPere excelled at playing the spoons participating in the celebration.
Lifting the spirits and energy of the people with his rapid vibrations.
He used two steel tablespoons held in one hand with a finger in between,
So that the spoon bowls could hit each other making the sound of a tambourine.
Hitting one hand above the spoons and then his leg or sides of his body,
In time to the fiddlers loosened up the spirits and enlivened everybody.

They played a joyful song that was over three hundred years old,
Which had more than one hundred known verses so I am told.
It was sung by the voyageurs paddling in a sixteen man canoe.
Who enlivened their journey with the song that they all knew.

V'LA L'BON VENT	English Translation
CHORUS:	CHORUS
V'la l'bon vent, v'la l'joli vent	"Here is the good wind, here is the pretty wind"
V'la l'bon vent m'amie m'appelle	"Here is the good wind my friend calls me
V'la l'bon vent, v'la l'joli vent	"Here is the good wind, here is the pretty wind"
V'la l'bon vent m'amie m'attend	"Here is the good wind my friend calls me
1. Derrière chez nous y'a un étant (2X)	Behind my house there is a pond
Derrière chez nous y'a un étant	Behind my house there is a pond

(2X)	
Trois beaux canards s'en vont baignant	Where three little ducks went for a swim
Trois beaux canards s'en vont baignant	Where three little ducks went for a swim
2. Le fils du roi s'en va chassant (2X)	Son of a king went out hunting
Le fils du roi s'en va chassant	Son of a king went out hunting
Avec son grand fusil d'argent	With his long silver gun
Avec son grand fusil d'argent	With his long silver gun
3. Visa le noir, tua le blanc	Aimed at the black, killed the white
Visa le noir, tua le blanc	Aimed at the black, killed the white
Oh fils du roi, tu est méchant	Son of a king, you rotten scoundrel
Oh fils du roi, tu est méchant	Son of a king, you rotten scoundrel
D'avoir tuer mon canard blanc	For having shot my white duck

This song was also a chansons répondre (response songs) where one sang a line,
Which was then repeated by everyone else who was singing by design.
This allowed everyone gathered in the room to join in the fun and belong,
Without first having to know any or all of the words or verses of the song.
The energy in the room soared when people danced the gigue (jig),
Enthusiastic step dancing in couples soon crowded the floor, real big.

This style of dancing included lively music called jigs and reels,
Had dancers wearing leather shoes with metal clickers on toes and heels.
It's lively skipping, stepping and tapping footwork on the wooden floor,
With spurts of aggressive unexpected energy which we could not ignore.
The musicians repertoire had reels, polkas, foxtrots, waltzes and tunes,
Accompanied by accordion, harmonica, fiddles and metal spoons.

The harmonica reel à bouche (mouth music) added interesting chromatic notes,
While spoons and foot tapping provided the percussion for the dancing folks.
Occasionally each couple danced the gigue one at a time taking a turn,
And at other times they danced solo almost in competition, a win to earn.
The gigue is the traditional dance and with its music forms a perfect harmony,
Enthusiastically performed in a jovial environment very remarkably.

Well fortified with food and all warmed up, on the fiddle and accordion music we rely,
Having eaten too much we energetically dance aiming our digestion to satisfy.
The fiddlers accompanied by harmonica and the accordion play many reels,
The happy dancing couples swing and twirl going round in circular wheels.
The rhythmic foot taping by the musicians adds to the percussion for the tune,
The merriment continues through the night and it will be morning soon.

Christmas day started rather early as children woke up at day break,
While most of the party goers were pretty tired but were mostly awake.
At the prospect of expectation of wonderful gifts and toys they were excited,
Gift opening time was the most magical moment and they were delighted.
GrandPere proudly sat there revelling in their joy and smiling faces,
At times he laughed so hard while clutching his suspender braces.

Cleaning away the torn wrappings, then it was time for Christmas dinner,
Oysters, escargots, and smoked salmon as appetizers were a good beginner.
The family members with renewed appetites bowed their heads in expectation,
While the excited and delighted children prepared for their recitation.
To say thanks for the Christmas dinner the custom was to choose a child,
Who always approached the task hesitantly while everyone else smiled.

A seven-year-old boy was given the task. He thanked his family,
His parents aunts and uncles, cousins and God for the food happily.
He gave thanks for the turkey, the stuffing, even the cranberry sauce,

The tourtiere, the pea soup and then came a long wait and a pause.
Everyone waited ... and waited and looked to see what was wrong,
But they saw him deep in thought but his resolve was strong.

He looked up at his mother and asked in desperation almost crying,
"If I thank God for the Brussels sprouts, won't he know that I'm lying?"
We had turkey, gravy and trimmings, vegetables and maple tasting baked beans,
Different flavoured quiches, a "plateau de fromages" (cheeses) and greens.
For dessert we had la bûche de Noël not as cake but in ice cream form,
Chocolates, marrons glacés (candied chestnuts), crème brûlée while still warm.

After Christmas day the festivities go on with Le Jour de L'an, New Years Day,
New Year's Eve is typically spent with family and friends and it is common to say.
Wishing, "Je te souhaite beaucoup d'amour, d'amitié, de santé et de la prospérité",
I wish you much love, friendship, health, and prosperity, bonne année.
With the Christmas tree bending under the weight of its decorations,
The custom continues to be passed on to each successive generation.

The frantic activity in the kitchen goes on with preparations,
That involve careful planning of delicious foods and libations.
Just before New Years at the boucherie (butcher's) meat counter,
A woman was trying to find a turkey that was bigger and rounder.
In desperation she asked the butcher if the turkeys got any bigger?
'No, madam,' sorrowfully he replied, 'they're all dead', what a kicker!

New Year's Day (le Jour de l'An) is a national holiday celebrated on January first,
Marked by having a Réveillon feast with a champagne toast to quench the thirst.
The celebration can be a simple, intimate dinner with family and friends,
Or, une soirée dansante, (a dance party) on circumstances it all depends.
New Year's Eve, in memory of a pope is also known as la Saint-Sylvestre,
And is celebrated with a feast, le Réveillon de la Saint-Sylvestre as a gesture

In many churches on New Year's Eve Special services to thank God are held,
For the gifts which God has given them in the past year and at which they marvelled.
And to implore His blessings and pray for necessary graces in the forthcoming year,
Prayers and toasts concerning gratefulness for the past year's blessings, very sincere.
Hope and luck for the future, and thanking guests for their New Year's camaraderie,
Further marked by fireworks, parades, and looking ahead the future to foresee.

On New Year's Day best wishes are exchanged; everyone is included big and small,
Hospitality is a hallmark of the evening with sincere friendly spirit embracing all.
Family spirit, love and kindness to family patriarchs and matriarchs is displayed,
No one is excluded from family festivities on New Year's Eve, isolation is forbade.
The parish priest, as our Spiritual Father, at the Mass, gave his blessing to everyone,
And he reminded the fathers to bestow their blessing on their families as he had done.

On New Year's morning the father always blessed the children we discover,
And the tradition has been lovingly passed on from one generation to another.
In Christian families the New Year paternal blessing was obligatory from long ago,
A unifying and loving expression that some people have decided to forego.
The blessing was a way to start the year well by putting yourself under divine protection.
And fostering a strong familial bonding and unselfish sharing of parental affection.

The paternal blessing (La Bénédiction Paternelle) of New Year's Day began at dawn
As suggested by their mother, children asked their father to bless them as they yawn.
In the kitchen or the living room the family settles in and are quiet and still,
Everyone is awake, some only half dressed and youngest in dishabille.

They are shy and timid at the suggestion and hesitate but do as they are told,
They go to him and get on their knees with hands in prayer they uphold.

The father standing raises his right hand and the sign of the cross he makes,
This blessing gesture made with nobility, a tear in his eye, he undertakes.
Saying, "I bless you, dear children, wishing you much health, happiness, and again,
A good year in the name of the Father and of the Son and of the Holy Spirit. Amen."
"Je vous souhaite une bonne et heureuse année, une bonne santé el le paradis a la fin
De vos jours! Que Dieu vous bénisse au nom du Pere et du Fils et du Sainte Esprit. Amen".

The moment was charged with great emotion; an important time of reflection for all.
He invites his children to stand up and embraces them, the big, the short and the tall.
It was a moment of great pride for him, a sign of recognition of his worth,
A sacred moment welding the family was a testimony of his faith on earth.
This ritual at this time of year is aimed to strengthen family ties,
While dissipating the grudges and the rivalries and relationships to revitalize.

On New Year's Day families visited their grandparents and as soon as they arrived,

The children and grandchildren went together to GrandPere; their visit highly prized.
The old uneducated man, strong as an oak, had laboured hard and survived,
Neatly combed and shaved wearing his big strap suspenders, with them he thrived.
For everyone, it is an unforgettable moment as he gives them his blessing,
He pronounces his simple wishes as tears flow on his cheeks he was suppressing.

In families where the father was absent, the duty was performed by the eldest son,
Rarely did the role fall to the mother or the eldest if it was a girl, just was not done.
Where distance separated the family the father still gave his blessing by telephone.
The moment remains intimate and privileged among those to whom it is well known.
It was customary for the children and grandchildren to go to the oldest male,
Usually the grandfather on New Years to receive their blessing without fail.

The holiday period ends on January 6 with the celebration of Epiphany,
It's called Jour des Rois, which has a special cake to mark the time cheerfully.
A traditional flat pastry cake, la galette des rois, is made of two sheets of puff pastry,
Filled with frangipane (almond paste) with a treat hidden inside and is very tasty.
Whomever finds the treat becomes king or queen and gets to wear a gold paper crown,
And chooses his or her partner for the evening and is the talk of the town.

I learned that New Year's Day celebration is called Le Réveillon du St. Sylvestre,
And of course all kinds of traditional foods are prepared, what a gesture!
St. Sylvester, was a pope and New Year's Eve is his Roman Catholic feast day,
It starts on New Year's Eve and partying starts at midnight a gala soiree.
Lots of good food begins with the traditional appetizer of wholesome pea soup,
Then the main dish of tourtière is served causing everyone at the table to regroup.

Sometimes the order is reversed, turkey with cranberries and gravy is served,
Or it's a stew made with pork hocks (ragoût de patte de cochon) has been observed.
So the tourtière with cinnamon and cloves is brought out later, along with the dessert,
Then back to enjoying more of the main dishes causing many of us to revert.
We savour the seasoned finely ground pork dissolving in our mouth,
Eyeing the tarte au sucre (sugar pie) and the bûche de Noël (yule log) no doubt.

The tarte made with maple syrup and the log covered with chocolate frosting.
Some are partying, drinking and with the music are dancing and waltzing.
After the dessert, to complete the celebratory meal, bubbly champagne abounds,
While friendly warm best wishes, hugs and kisses make their rounds.
The New Year is brought in with joy and excitement and energetic musicians,
Elder members of the family blessing the children as one of the traditions.

Canvassing house to house we have La Guignolée practiced by young men
Singing songs and asking for donations to help the poor there and then.
On Epiphany (6 January) the galette des rois, a puff pastry cake is shared,
Celebrating the arrival of the Three Wise Men in Bethlehem, it declared.
Filled with frangipane, (sweet almond cream), with a small fève, (charm) inside.
A cardboard crown accompanies the cake for the charm finder to confide.

And crown the finder's chosen person to be his or her queen or king,
Everyone gathers to cut the famous cake and see what luck will bring.
The flaky puff galette fillings can vary adding new tastes to the tradition,
Almond cream flavoured with Grand Marnier and candied orange are one edition.
Others delicately flavoured with Bourbon vanilla, with apricots, figs, honey and spices,
Filled with a creamy ganache made for everyone to delight in its slices.

Everyone laughed learning the story of Filbert's talk with Raymond and his response,
Wandering what payment his dad would exact for Yvon with such nonchalance.
Marie was furious with her father for listening to such malicious untruthful gossip,
That some person had spread for some crazy unknown purpose to profit.
Marie's boyfriend Yvon was the love of her life and she was planning to be his wife,
They were simply planning their engagement and marriage without any strife.

Marie said her father Filbert should have had trusted her and Yvon with a better view,
Yvon and Marie devout Catholics would never have indulged such a sin to construe.
Filbert was taken in by some silly fool and to everyone he profusely apologized,
Promising that he would never doubt them again and try his most to be wise.
The Curée restored calm and peace and encourage Filbert not to moralize,
In the spirit of renewal at New Years relationships he helped to harmonize.

The Curée's homily focused on Luke 6:37 "Judge not, and you will not be judged",
"Can a blind man lead a blind man? Will they not both into a pit be plunged?
Condemn not, and you will not be condemned; are eternal lessons from heaven,
Saying it's important to remember, "Forgive, and you will be forgiven".
He illustrated the message with a story from a man with a near death experience,
The man Lionel, who while in hospital with a serious illness was partly delirious.

Lionel said he was shocked and bewildered as he entered Heaven's door,
Not by the beauty of it all, nor by the bright lights or its décor..
But it was the folks in Heaven Who made him sputter and gasp,
The thieves, the liars, the sinners, the alcoholics and the trash.
There stood the boy from school who cheated and stole money! Twice.
Next to him was his old neighbor who never said anything nice.

Jean Marie, who he always thought was rotting away in hell,

Was sitting pretty on a puffy cloud, looking incredibly well.
God must've made a mistake. He asked Jesus, 'Help me to discern,
How'd all these sinners get up here? Would love to hear, to learn.
And why's everyone so quiet, So somber – give me a clue."
"Hush, child," He replied, "No one thought they'd be seeing you."

After the festivities life returned to normal and Sylvio the dépanneur was busy,
GrandPere and I visit often, sit around to get warm when the days are dreary.
Sylvio's wife, Margaret when home after teaching school is a real pleasure,
She shared her story about Jean Paul whose mother was pregnant, a treasure.
The concerned little boy asked, "What's in your stomach, Mother?"
She looked at the sweet innocent child with a smile she replied, "It's your brother".

The next day in school as part of our lesson I asked, "Who has little brother or sister?"
Many hands went up but Jean Paul said, "I have a brother but my mother ate him."
Teaching math she asked, "If you had one piastre and you asked your father for one,
How many piastres would you have?" One hand went up. Vincent said, "One."
I said Vincent "You don't know your arithmetic, I said if you ask him for another.
How many piastres would you have?" Vincent said, "One! You don't know my father."

108

4. Good Fortune

It would be unforgiveable and very remiss, indeed thoughtless, of me not to record my warm welcome upon arrival and good fortune in meeting GrandPere and having him as chaperone, guide and most of all a true friend during my visit. He introduced me to his family, his gracious wife Marie-Rose whom I also referred to as GrandMere. I met all fourteen of their children, their spouses and even their grandchildren. GrandPere was a retired dairy farmer whose children complained that he wasn't retired enough. He insisted on doing chores saying that it kept him young. The reason for my not writing about my welcome is that it left a somewhat embarrassing although lasting impression on my memory as described in this chapter.

At first being firmly reluctant to record my smelly, foul smelling ordeal,
Thinking about it, I would have hidden the love shown to me that I feel.
Dear Reader I apologize if the described mess is hard to endure,
But I did arrive and found a precious friendship by falling in cow manure.
I hope that on your life's journey you don't fall into the ignoring trap,
Of not looking for that glistening diamond even in a piece of crap.

I had made reservations at the Auberge; I flew and then arrived by train,
To experience what snow was like, my curiosity I could hardly contain.
I was met at the station by a kindly old gent who was named GrandPere,
The auberge had sent him to get me as he did others part of his affaire.
J'peux-tu t'aider, mon gars? (Can I help you, my boy?) said he with a grin,
In the cold wind with those words our wonderfully warm friendship would begin.

Not knowing exactly what he meant my phrasebook I had to withdraw.
I embarked unto his horse drawn sleigh and lots of snow I saw,
Pis, t'aimes-tu mon char? Si t'as frette, dis-moé-lé, gêne-toé pas!
(So do you like my vehicle? If you're cold let me know, don't be shy),
I covered up with the blanket and murmured something didn't know why,
He said it would give him a chance to talk anglais (english) me to terrify.

His English was a thousand time better than my French phrasebook was for me,
From my futile attempts he could see that I was truly begging for mercy.
GrandPere said not to worry we would get to the auberge and as a choice,
If I wanted he would be glad to give me a tour while he practiced his voice.
He did not have a chance to speak English very often as he would have liked,
And he talked about his family and proposed I visit them and gave me an invite.

I checked in at the auberge, the people knew GrandPere very well,
He helped bring my luggage up to my room and bid me farewell.
I asked GrandPere if he really meant what he had said about the invite,
He was sincere and asked if I would be interested in meeting everyone that night.
With the wind blowing fiercely some company would help spark my appetite,
I answered graciously thanking him with great expectations and delight.

The sleigh ride to his home was a glistening and an exhilarating ride,
Over snow blowing hills and valleys with lots of fir trees along the countryside.
He told me that his wife's name was Marie-Rose and they had 14 children,
He said he enjoyed the challenge of speaking English whenever he can.
We arrived and I kissed his wife on both cheeks saying Bonjour,
Having read in a book that it was the custom to be followed but I was unsure.

I was welcomed in fact warmly received and repeatedly asked if I was hungry,
GrandPere offered me some what he called Caribou which I accepted humbly.
I told them about life back home in broken French and how I wondered about snow,
Their English was much better than I could express myself in the French I know.
But we understood one another really well and GrandMere insisted I stay for souper.
While still hours away, GrandPere was getting ready to look after the horse and sleigh.

It all started with (Will you help me, my boy) Tu peux m'aider , mon gars?
I agreed, not knowing what he was up to, and I wondered with awe.
He followed with (Put on your hat it's cold outside) Mets ta tuque, y fait frette!
We headed to the barn for an awesome experience I will never forget.
It was occupied by milk cows, was warm, well lit and kept very clean,
The cows were in pens with feed spread in front with lots of hay on the scene.

This was the cows home from December to March kept out of the cold,
What struck me most was the strong stinky smell that was so bold.
Some smells give you a headache some cause a gag reflex and you hold your breath,
It didn't help much I craved for some air, not breathing can cause your death.
This unforgettable smell of ammonia, methane forever lingers in my memory,
With tears in my eyes, I listened to how these animals had won first prix.

GrandPere told me that the average cow is (544.8 kg) or 1,200 lbs. in weight,
With a life span of roughly 18 years, but some between 25-30 will gravitate.
Her first calf she has when two years old and then has milk for her baby,
A cow produces an average of 8 gallons (30.1 liters) of milk daily.
A gallon of milk weighs 8.6 lbs. so 8 gallons weigh 68.8 lbs. in weight
Some breeds may produce from 4 to 20 gallons (15.1-7.5 liters) at any given date.

It happened so suddenly' tail to the side, brown fecal matter came pouring out,
It splattered on the ground much like soft ice cream from a machine spout.
I slipped and fell and down I went; he said that I was not careful, I did not look,
I was shocked by the efficiency of the process, the pile and the little time it took.
I don't know what I expected but I was in the thick of a sticky, stinking mess,
How was I ever going to recover my distress and at supper was to impress?

I desperately tried to get up and outstretched my arm and put my hand in still more,
Losing my balance I sat firmly on the warm slippery, slimy paddy on the floor.
I took his hand with mine covered with goo and sheepishly got up wiping my face,
Only now to find that I had smeared the stinky brown goo all over the place.
GrandPere said, J'en parle avec humour, mais on est vraiment dans la merde,
(I treat the subject in a humorous way, but we are really in the shit) he declared.

He continued, Coudon, t'es ben ben magané! (Jeez, you're in really rough shape!),
Covered in the foul smelling stinking crap I felt trapped, no way to escape.
I felt terrible and told GrandPere how very sorry that I was such a dumb clutch,

"Think nothing of it", he said, "remember I got some too after your hand I touch."
(You have to do the best you can), It faut se débrouiller, faire le mieux qu'on peut,
(You are not alone, we are two). Vous n'êtes pas seul; maintenant nous sommes deux.

Negative thoughts entered my mind inviting gray clouds over my head,
Making me very anxious, in a panic filled with lots of stress and dread.
J'ai la tête pleine de merde !   My brain has just turned to shit,
I fought hard and realized that these crazy thoughts I had to quit.
This experience had to be a challenge for me. an opportunity to learn,
I looked for the something that would be meaningful for me in return.

"When life gives you lemons, make lemonade" was a thought that came to mind,
A thought that with GrandPere's earlier statement was well aligned.
It was difficult to anticipate the best possible outcome against the worst,
Especially so when deeply in a filthy, shitty mess a person is immersed.
Would I be sitting naked for supper or possibly be uninvited my mind ran,
Worst arriving naked at the auberge; expecting the best but I needed a plan.

GrandPere led me to one side and took the water hose and I got a cold shower,
I think that the water just gave the mess a boost in smelly, stinking power.
He got all of the stuff off me and my clothes; but like a rat I was soaking wet,
Give me your wet clothes, use the horse blanket he ordered and left something to get.
Some towels and dry clothes he brought back, even several pairs of shoes,
Sous-vêtements longue or long underwear he wanted me to choose.

Suggesting a one piece with a 2 button square drop hatch I could not refuse,
This everyone wore under their clothes he said, the cold it subdues.
It was body fitted with long legs and long sleeves and buttons in the front.
Wondering if normal body functions would be impeded or required a stunt,
Never having seen one I thankfully accepted without question or any excuse.
I quickly dressed hugging the warm clothes, the cold shivers to diffuse.

With the cold shower and all of the activity to get warm and to dress,
My depressing negative thoughts vanished along with feelings of distress.
We bundled my wet clothes which he said that his wife would look after,
And we looked at the mess and loudly filled the barn with laughter.
I was wearing clothes from his boys and his son Camille's shoes,
And experiencing a formidable kindness that I simply could not refuse.

I thought about the saying, of understanding when walking in another person's shoes,
How important it is to walk beside someone else, and see things from their views.
It would have been easy to laugh about my situation and let me sit on the shelf,
He understood what I was undergoing as if he had undergone it before by himself.
Obviously what it felt like to be me covered in merde, GrandPere knew,
He assessed my situation with compassion and knew exactly what to do.

GrandPere said, "A cow pooping shock people not familiar with cows,
I see that you have never before been in a cow pasture or barn to browse.
Cows don't think about it, or make any arrangements, they just go,
Ejecting suddenly and efficiently at any time rewarding you with a gateaux.
They all do it anywhere and the others are only too happy to walk in it",
Cow plops tend to be evenly distributed wherever they are, I admit.

Laughing he said, " Nous sautons sur les bouses de rennes, claires et foncées",
(We jump over light and dark pieces of cow shit) life goes on hoping for no replay.
GrandPere told me that a cow can pee up to ten and poop up to 15 times a day,
Producing 65 lbs. (29.5 kg) of feces or manure like an assembly line without delay.
Manure production (65 lbs.) rivals that of milk (68.8 lbs) each day,
Add 3.5 gal. (13.2 liters) of urine per day; almost striking equilibrium either way.

People caring for cattle build up a lifetime of immunity to manure smells,
Manure odour from grass-fed cattle is different than from corn-fed cattle he tells.
Studying the shape, size, color and texture of cow pies you find out the diet quality,

When to supplement feeding, or rotate to a different pasture; applied technology.
To promote milk production and maintain body condition when cows are lactating
Cows can become sick, have hoof problems by standing in their own filth stagnating.

Think about it, one cow produces 12 tons (908 kg) of manure a year,
And it becomes a real environmental challenge to make it all disappear.
Time is lost cleaning dirty, poop-crusted cows off before each milking,
Adding to air pollution by stinking ammonia and nitrogen gas they bring.
Just then some of his family arrived at the barn, it was cow milking time,
For this they all pitched in every day in the morning and before suppertime.

I met three of his sons; Camille, Raymond and Roger and a daughter, Laurette,
One of whom said, "Il fait un froid de canard" ("Make a duck cold") I will forget.
The expression has nothing to do with ducks, it means "it's extremely cold."
And GrandPere explained about my slippery mishap, they were all told,
The cows marched into the milking parlour where milking machines were attached,
And milk to the refrigerated milk tank was very efficiently dispatched.

The milking parlour has cows walk onto a raised platform with gates,
While milking, the gate keeps the cow from moving; a safe area it creates.
The cows udder is disinfected and dried before attaching the device,
All four suction cylinders of the milking machine are attached to be precise.
A hose runs from the milking machine to an overhead steel pipeline,
Running the length of the barn it is connected to a big bulk tank by design.

Before milking machines, only about 6 cows per hour could be milked,
Now, in one hour about 100 cows are milked when machines are equipped.
Dairy cows are milked twice a day using these vacuum milking machines,
Through steel pipes to a refrigerated bulk milk tank the raw milk convenes.
Cooled to 40° F (4.4° C), awaiting a refrigerated truck within a few hours,
Delivered to the milk processing plant, the milk is fresh and never sours..

GrandPere said that Daniel, Gaston the mécanicien's ten year-old son, visited the farm,
"He watched me attach the milking suction devices on the cow with no harm".
Daniel said "Wow! You're going to jump-start her the way Papa starts a car!"
I am sure that it is something Daniel will long remember as part of his histoire.
When milking is over, the cow walks out the other side I was advised,
After every milking, all milk contact services are washed, rinsed and sanitized.

GrandPere said he still remembers the first time he saw a cow poop when he was three,
Cows "poop and pee" a lot--once about every 20 minutes as a regular frequency.
I was most grateful to GrandPere for giving me a shower and warm clothes,
A kindness I knew that I could never repay; even though he delivered it by hose.
My slimy calamity about which I was so reluctant to write and describe,
Was second nature to them and did not leave any of them amused or horrified.

I got the impression that a similar occurrence or even worse they all had,
This experience we all shared and in a very personal way it made me glad.
I found comfort knowing that others understood my struggle,
Had been there, too, made me feel less alone giving me a chuckle.
They were very supportive; I felt worthy that friends I had secured,
Despite the added work and my complaining that they endured.

To a dairy farmer a cow's manure's texture and consistency although unappealing,
Helps them identify cow ailments and is a key indicator of their health and well being.
Compared to other "industrial products" manure is better than gold and is profuse,
Besides milk, manure correctly handled is the most valuable thing that cows produce.
Farmers know that manure increases crop and milk yields by enriching the soil.
Over 100 pounds of manure each day from an 800-pound cow makes farmers toil.

Fields coated with fresh manure "smell like money" makes dairy farmers smile,
Preparing for winter they compost cow manure in a humongous well drained pile.
During the spring and summer most of it is spread on their pastures and hoed,
Some of it is sold in bulk to visitors, friends and neighbors by the pickup load.
Some exchange a cord or two of cut and split firewood for a truck load of manure,
Each fall or spring the compost is spread on gardens, abundant vegetables to ensure.

With boots on, standing in the barn's gutter shovelling poop and pee,
Farmers don't see or smell manure, they see and smell a valuable commodity.
There is always lots of work to do including maintaining the long dirt road,
And repairing washouts after a torrential downpour and where landslides flowed.
Plowing snow all winter long and spreading sand when roads turn to solid ice,
To protect travellers who dare to venture out against the best advice.

Cold weather involves more animal care like preparing warm meals for the hens,
Keeping all creatures warm and cow's drinking water from freezing in their pens.
From April to September farmers cut, split and stack wood for winter and for buyers,
In hot and dry summers they watch and try to prevent devastating wildfires.
They mend fences, plant bushes and trees preventing erosion which they abhor,
Refreshing the soil with nutrients so that soil fertility they can restore.

To avoid water table damage the abundant manure has to be managed every day,
The effort expended is massive and the results it offers must repay.

Farmers can't afford to be squeamish, even the stink of manure they learn to adore,
L'idée est ici pour le dire en termes imagés de transformer de la merde en or.
(The idea here, to put it in graphic terms for once, is to turn shit into gold),
To collect, pile, compost, refine, enrich, package, market and then to be sold.

GrandPere told me how innovative the good notary Jean Marc was last summer,
As part of the village's festival amidst the renovation of the Centre d'Accueil clamour.
He organized a fundraising activity he called Tarte aux Vaches (Cow Pie) Bingo game,
By promoting it, making a success, their large financial shortfall they overcame.
He sold four tickets for each square at rates of $10, $20, $50 and $100 detailed below,
People from all over came; prizes won were $500; $1,000; $2500; $5,000 très beau.

Jean Marc announced the time and place of the Tarte aux Vaches Bingo event,
Notices were posted everywhere and even announced in church with their consent.
A 100' x 120' field grid was marked off with construction paint in 10' X 12' squares,
For a total of 100 squares with all being of equal shape, size and equal shares.
The field grid (and cow) was protected from interference from spectators by a fence,
No one was permitted and interference with the progress of the event was an offence.

$500 was the prize for the ticket holder of the 'square on which the cow pie landed,
Where not all square tickets were sold, 50% of those sold was to be handed.
Tickets for up to 100 squares were quickly sold for $10.00 each one,
Proceeds after expenses were shared with the sponsors of the fun.
People selected their own lucky square ticket, and their name was recorded,
This was diligently verified when the winning prize was awarded.

A cutoff date for ticket sales was set after which no tickets were sold,
A list of ticket holders was posted at the Centre d'Accueil for everyone to behold.
At the announced time a cow was led into the grid area and allowed to freely roam,
Until a cow pie or "plop" landed on a square, not cow pee, just cow pie alone.
If the "plop" landed on several squares, the winner was the square with the most.
Taking into consideration width and depth as the line judge had diagnosed.

If the "plop" landed on an unsold square the adjacent ticket holders stood to win,
Providing that at least one full side of their square was shared therein.
This could end up being more than one winner, up to, but not more than four,
Who would then share in the prize money equally, that's for sure.
Square ticket holders did not need to be present to win, the winner would be contacted,
The winner was responsible for any associated fees/taxes so as not to be misled.

Winners had to provide proof of ticket ownership to claim their prize,
They had 30 days to claim the prize money as the rules clarified.
Unclaimed prize monies were donated to the church that's how it was handled.

If a "plop" was not placed within 3 hours the planned event was declared cancelled.
At last the moment arrived, spectators held their breath, until the cow splatted a pile,
Everyone waited……and……nothing happened; Ok it does sometimes take a while.

The good notary Jean Marc tried his best to cover all eventualities just in case,
Stipulating that the decision of the event judge(s), was final no one could erase.
If the event be cancelled a randomly selected attendee was to draw the winning ticket,
And have the same result or outcome as though the planned event had actually existed.
But inevitably the swift elimination occurred to everyone's satisfaction and elation,
They were rewarded with a cascading flow, a "plop" and an aromatic aeration.

GrandPere told me about the Vache Canadienne cow bred in French Canada,
From imported Brittany and Normandy cattle around 1660 with lots of stamina.
The Canadienne is a hardy dairy breed able to withstand Quebec's climatic conditions,
Having inherited resilience and robustness, alertness and quick of temper traditions.
To variations in temperature and walking on rugged terrain it adapts really well,
Remaining on pasture for longer periods of time in early spring and late fall they excel.

These qualities have vested the Canadienne with a longer lifespan too.
Birthing requiring no assistance and a shorter interval between calvings, also true.
The breed possesses good fertility and a legendary ease of calving care,
Having healthy producing fifteen-year-old cows was not rare.
However Government milk payment system emphasized volume and quantity,
Instead of quality farmers were encouraged to switch breeds as Government policy.

By the mid 1880's, the breed was almost lost, it was facing extinction,
In 1895 French Canadian Cattle Breeder's Association prevented that distinction.
In 1901 the breed was recognized in New York as the most profitable dairy breed,
In the 1970s milk production again caused the government to intercede.
And encouraged uncontrolled interbreeding with Brown Swiss, more milk to produce,
The tendency then was the Canadienne breed to further reduce.

In 1999, the Government of Quebec gave the Canadienne cow official heritage status,
Effectively stopping the introduction and use of Brown Swiss genetics apparatus.
Attempting to preserve the purity of Canadienne cattle and they further supported,
A breeding program to preserve the breed; thus extinction was thwarted.
An initiative by farmers working hard to save the purebred breed is underway, voila,
It's the Association for the Development of the Canadienne Cattle Breed in Charlevoix.

The Canadienne cow breed tends to be of small to medium-size,
Cows weigh between 400 to 500 kg and bulls about 800 kg. no surprise.
If horns are present, they are long and upturned with darker coloured tips,
A cow produces 27 litres of wholesome milk from two daily milking trips.
For a rough average of 5000 kg of milk, as a normal function,
Which with 4.3% butterfat and 3.6% protein is perfect for cheese production.

There is an average of 50 to 55 cows in a usual dairy farm,
An average herd, has 1 bull to every 30 cows sharing his charm.
Each day in addition to moisture in their feed, silage, or grass;
Cows drink between 25 to 50 gallons (80 to 180 litres) of water mass.
And they eat around 40 to 100 pounds (45 kg) of grass like alfalfa a day;
When grass is not available then about 35 lbs. (11 kg) of good hay.

Also about 16 kgs of grain; corn, soybeans, wheat, barley or oats is a must,
Mix is ground up and moistened with molasses to keep down the dust;
Add about 11 kgs of vegetables, fruit, cabbage, potatoes, apples and beets,

Turnips, carrots, broccoli, pea vines, pumpkins, squash all fine eats.
Add to the mix about 2 kgs of protein supplement; minerals and salt,
Cows simply adore licking a salt block or granules without finding any fault.

Corn for feed is planted in the spring and harvested in the fall complete,
Although it looks the same as the sweet corn-on-the-cob people eat.
It is harder and can't be cooked or eaten; It is usually ground and mixed,
With barley or oats, plus vitamins and minerals, a protein food is fixed.
Stored in the silo, wet corn ferments making it tastier and easier to digest by the way,
This "pickling" process makes grass more palatable and is used for wet hay.

A cow encircles grass with her tongue; with her bottom teeth she cuts it off underneath.
She then swallows it without chewing. since in front she has no top teeth.
Cows are cud chewing mammals; like sheep and camels they are called ruminant,
Cow stomachs are divided into four digestive compartments, a real processing plant.
The rumen, reticulum, omasum and abomasum have a specific role to start,
In digesting cellulose; food barely chewed enters the rumen the first and largest part.

Up to 50 gallons of this cud is thus held; next the reticulum pushes the unchewed food,
Back up the esophagus and into the mouth where it is rechewed for an interlude.
A cud of food is chewed with teeth set back in her jaw as many as 60 times they say.
A cow chews her cud (regurgitated, partially digested food) for up to 8 hours each day.
After re-chewing, or rumination, the food eventually passes through the omasum,
The omasum filters out the water, breaks down the food and more nutrients are wrung.

Finally, the food enters the abomasum, like a human stomach by the way,
Cattle produce 500 to 1,000 liters of methane gas each and every day.
Cows have 32 teeth; 6 molars on the top and bottom of each side,
8 incisors on the bottom front; a tough pad of skin but no teeth on the top front inside.
Dairy animal names change as they grow older; a calf is a bovine newborn,
A heifer is a young female for which a calf has yet to be born.

A bull is a mature male bovine whereas a mature female bovine is a cow,
Cows can live to the age of 25 years old if people would allow.
Just like people, cows are pregnant for 9 months and their milk output ceases,
In order to grow her calf, two months before giving birth giving milk decreases.
During this period the cow is known as a Dry Cow by the vet's staff,
Cows give milk for about ten months (or about 305 days) after having a calf.

A cow's mood barometer is said by many people to be the tail,
But a wagging tail does not mean that a happy cow will prevail.
Crabby cows are caused by dinner off schedule, calves bellowing and other reasons,
Not being milked in a timely fashion and annoying flies depending on the seasons.
A cow must have a calf in order to produce milk it appears,
From then on cows are milked for an average of 3-4 years.

The average cow is 2 years old when she has her first calf.
Calves are fed milk until they are 8-9 weeks old at most 9 and a half.
Dairy cows provide 90% of the world's milk supply.
There are two breeds; Holsteins and Jerseys on which farmers rely,
The best cows give over 25 gallons of milk each day.
That equates to 400 glasses of milk by the way.

A cow gives an average of 2,000 gallons of milk per year.
That's over 30,000 glasses of milk it would appear.
Holsteins are black and white, and each has a unique pattern.
A Holstein calf at birth weighs 80-110 lbs while a cow weighs 1,300-1,500 lbs. we learn.
Jerseys vary from dark brown or fawn, and sometimes are splashed with white arrays,
A Jersey calf at birth is 60 lbs. while 900-1,000 lbs. is what a cow weighs.

The average body temperature of a cow is 101.5 Farenheit or 38.6 Celsius degrees,
In an average herd for every 30 cows there is one bull, their needs to appease.

To protect a calf's health separate living quarters ensuring the best care is prime,
To build up newborn calves immune systems requires proper nourishment and time.
It is best for newborns that they are not exposed to environmental germs,
Or germs that can be passed on from older animal concerns.

To ensure their health, newborn calves often by bottle are fed,
Two to four quarts of colostrum, the first milk produced is given instead.
Colostrum is high in fat, protein and antibodies essential for a calf we are told,
Calves are fed from the cow until they are between 8 and 9 weeks old.
About 12 to 14 months after her previous calf, a cow will again give birth,
A young female calf is called a heifer until she has her first calf to roam the earth..

A young male is called a bull calf. Their own calves, cows never forget or disavows,
They even lick their grown calves just as when they were young and carouse.
Dairy cows can produce 125 pounds of saliva a day,
And up to 200 pounds of pungent flatus they also convey.
Of all milk breeds, the Holstein cow produces the most,
If people would let them, cows can live to the age of 25 years almost.

Cows can smell odours up to five or six miles away having a great sense of smell,
Cows can hear lower and higher frequencies better than humans just as well.
In a gallon of milk there are approximately 350 squirts,
Cows can pick and lick their noses with their tongues in regular spurts.
Each minute a cow's heart beats between 60 and 70 beats,
The average cow chews at least 50 times a minute when it eats.

Cows can't vomit but you can lead a cow upstairs,
However, cows knees can't bend properly to walk downstairs.
A Holstein's pattern is like a fingerprint all different spots,
No two cows have exactly the same pattern of black and white dots.
About 14 times a day regularly a cow stands up and sits,
A cow spends 10 to 12 hours a day lying down before it finally quits.

About four to 8 hours a day on average is what cows sleep,
Unlike horses, they don't sleep standing up and they don't cheat.

Cows are red-green colorblind but colours they do see,
In a bullfight, the waving cape attracts the bull not the red they all agree.

Cattle have almost 300 degrees of panoramic vision,
With blind spots right in front of and behind them with some provision.
Raw milk has harmful bacteria, is not safe and must be pasteurized,
Heating milk to 161 degrees Fahrenheit for more than 15 seconds is advised.
An average dairy cow weighs about 1,200 pounds,
And produces 70 lbs of milk; that's 8 gallons a day it abounds.

All of us, GrandPere; Camille, Raymond, Roger and Laurette,
Set off for home, they having completed their chores without a sweat.
The wind had picked up, howling, it was ushering in a storm,
We walked quickly through the drifts of snow soon to be warm.
Happy to arrive, greeted by appetizing aromas and soothing warm air,
I was really thankful although slightly itchy in my woolen long underwear.

I was introduced to more members of GrandPere's family,
I couldn't recall all of their names; it all happened too rapidly.
I know I met Giles, the barber and his wife Genevieve, GrandPere's daughter,
We were invited to sit at the table and I sat between Roger and his brother.
First on the table was fresh crusty baguette bread and creamy butter,
With a big bowl of thick delicious pea soup with Roger asking for another.

There was ham, potatoes, beans spinach, apple cider, milk and cheese,
GrandMere with daughters had prepared, everyone's hunger to appease.
The occasion gave everyone a chance to catch up on the news,
They exchanged their experiences, sharing each other's views.
GrandPere teased Genevieve about making rabbit's milk cheese,
Camille recounted the week's big public event in the diocese.

At the caisse populaire meeting important issues were being discussed,
Midway, a farmer's wife stood up and spoke her piece with some mistrust.
Taking exception an old farmer asked, "What does she know about anything whereas,
Very respectfully I ask, if she knows how many toes a pig has?"
Quick as a flash, red faced and with eyes glaring the woman replied,
"Take off your boots sir, and count them yourself!" she loudly cried.

Raymond asked, "Do you remember us purchasing a cow in St Eustache,
It was a long trip but we bought her for $200 she was a wonderful vache.
She produced lots of milk all of the time, and all of us were very happy,
To breed more like her we decided to buy a bull really strong and very classy.
Whenever the bull tried to mount the cow, the cow would move away,
No matter what approach the bull tried with the cow, there was no way.

At our wits end we decided to ask the Vet, who was very wise, what to do,
We told him how the cow always evaded the bull, everything that we knew.
Deep in thought the Vet asked, "Did you by chance, buy this cow in St Eustache?"
We were amazed, since we never mentioned where we bought the vache.
So we asked, "How did you know St Eustache is where we got the vache?"
The Vet replied with a distant look in his eye, "My wife is from St Eustache."

Genevieve's husband Giles, a sheep and goat farmer, was the only barber in town,
Some said he got his training from shearing the sheep that he had around.
He always had something startling or newsworthy to contribute,
Because in his shop he had heard many a tale and heated dispute.
His shop was a popular hangout for workmen engaged in their pursuit,
And for all shop keepers; this he heard from someone along the route.

Henri was driving a big truck across Canada with a load of live rabbits,
They were all loose in the trailer and not in cages against all of their habits.
Because of patches of ice he slid into the ditch, wide open went the doors,
The rabbits scurried everywhere, out of the truck into the great outdoors.
Sûreté du Québec (SQ) (Québec Provincial Police (QPP)) came to the scene,
The cop walked to the back of the truck finding Henri laughing unforeseen.

Henri lying on his back, arms flailing in the air, laughing hard as all hell,
The cop watched the pandemonium as the rabbits made their farewell,
The cop said, "Hey, your rabbits are loose, they're running everywhere",
Henri said, "They don't know where to go, I have the address, I declare."
The cop scratching his head was perplexed and decided to go away,
Henri was unhurt, not in distress the situation would handle itself anyway.

Camille added, "Remember old Louis buying a bull after getting a loan from the Caisse,

"How's our bull doing?" asked Hervé, the Caisse manager, days later visiting his place.
"Our bull is no good. He's out there in the pasture not performing and I am in debt."
Hervé, very serious, thoughtfully suggested, "You better call the vet."
A couple of days later, Hervé visited again and asked, "How's our bull doing now?"
Louis said, "Fantastic, done all of my cows and is now working on the neighbour's cow.

"He jumped the fence and even did the job at the other neighbours place",
Hervé is amazed and asks, "Wow, What did the Vet give him, good heavenly grace?"
Louis says, "He talked very calmly to him and gave him some pills."
Hervé says, "What kind of pills that the bull so ably his reputation fulfills?"
Louis says, "I don't know, but they tasted sort of like peppermint."
Hervé wondered why old Louis took a pill, but he got no hint.

The fromagerie is owned by GrandPere's daughter Genevieve a real connoisseur,
Her husband the barber, Giles, not Gilles, Gaspard's son, the raconteur.
Genevieve specializes in making wonderful cheese from different milk sources,
Using milk from goats, sheep and cows; winning awards she has many endorsers.
From goat milk she makes Chèvre; from sheep she makes Roquefort and Ossau,
GrandPere laughingly bugs her suggesting she try rabbit milk as something nouveau.

From cow milk she make Camembert, Brie, Cheddar and squeaky curd cheese,
They are all delicious and has no intention of adding despite his ongoing tease.
Cheese curds start off with pasteurized fresh milk and adding rennet the milk to clot,
The result is a mixture of whey and the early stages of the curd in the pot.
This is then cooked and is pressed to release the curd from the whey,
Thereby creating the final product of cheese curd ready to be given away.

Curds are firm and dense just like cheese, but with a springy, rubbery texture,
Their flavor is mild; against the teeth when bitten into, they release squeaking gesture.
Keeping them at room temperature can preserve their squeakiness,
After 12 hours, or refrigerated, cheese curds find their squeak to be less.
The demand for squeaky curd cheese has increased off the screen,
With the great popularity of french fries, gravy and curd cheese poutine.

Bacterial cultures are added giving cheese a different flavor formation,
They also acidify the milk, which aids in the curds coagulation.
Ricotta is the only exception made without cultures and is quite bland,
Okay for certain uses like spaghetti and dips to meet demand.
Regular cultures include yogurt, a heat loving culture that is used,
Buttermilk, a moderate temperature loving culture is also introduced.

There are many bacterial cultures in use that Genevieve prefers,
For squeaky cheese curds, heated goat milk or cow milk she stirs,
Adds her specialized bacterial culture allowing it to ripen for 1 hour to set.
She then adds rennet covering the pot for 45 minutes letting the milk to reset,
The curds are cut into 1/2" pieces with a stainless steel knife and left to rest.
Next for 20 minutes she cooks the curds stirring so not to make a sticky mess.

Then cools them pouring the curds into a colander with cold water where they drain,

She then breaks up the squeaky curds and salts to taste, deliciously hard to restrain.
Chèvre is a tart flavored cheese made from goat's milk favoured by those who are ill,
Often consumed by young children, the elderly, with low tolerance to cow's milk still.
Goat milk is more similar to human milk than that of the cow,
And much better for those who cannot tolerate cow milk anyhow.

Goat's milk with vinegar or lemon juice, curdles, is drained and pressed into curds,
The whey is used as animal feed or made into ricotta with added herbs.
For several days curds in cheesecloth bags are hung to drain and cure.
The soft goat cheese is then rolled and wrapped, its freshness and flavour to ensure.
Where the goat cheese is to be aged, it is first brined so as to form a rind,
It is then stored in a cool cheese cave for several months to cure as assigned.

Genevieve laughs every time she remembers a Sunday dinner many years ago,
When her parents invited the old Curée, this story she will not let her brother outgrow.
While they were in the kitchen preparing the meal; the Curée, she and Raymond,
Were in the salon (living room) the Curée very nicely asked Raymond alone.
What they were having for dinner that night? "Goat," little Raymond replied,
"Goat?" replied the Curée, "Are you sure about that?" he was mystified.

"Oui bien sur, (Yes for sure) I heard Dad say to Mom", Raymond deliver,
'Today is just as good as any to have the old goat for dinner.'
No goat was served; if the Curée had any doubts they were soon laid to rest,
The issue was never addressed perhaps the Curée was impressed.
Goat cheese does not melt like cow cheese does but it softens exposed to heat,
Firmer goat cheeses with rinds can be baked to form a warm almost creamy treat.

Log shaped Chèvre (goats cheese) is mild, crumbly and creamy when it is made,
A drier, firmer, flakier, and more acidic taste with age is portrayed.
Genevieve made two types of cheese from milk from sheep,
Roquefort is fudgy and has no rind is aged 2 to 4 months, left to reap.
Has green and blue veining tastes punchy, spicy-sweet, with incredible flavor,
That everyone favourably commenting with every bite that they savour

She also made Oussau a pressed, uncooked, raw sheep milk cheese of lush flavor,
Aged for about 90 days is mild, firm, smooth, sweet, and a little nutty layer upon layer.
It melts beautifully; and is frequently grated over pasta or soup,
Its flavour is hauntingly complex leaving people asking for another scoop.
From cow's milk Genevieve made Camembert, Brie, Cheddar and curds,
Her fromagerie has lots of daylight and is spotlessly clean one observes.

Camembert is a soft, creamy, surface-ripened cheese with remarkable reputations,
She uses pasteurized milk for reasons of safety and compliance with regulations.
The curd is cut into 1 cm (1/2 inch) cubes, salted, and put into molds to remain,
Where they are turned every six to twelve hours to allow the whey to drain.
After 48 hours, each mold has a flat, cylindrical, solid 250 grams (9 oz) cheese item,
That is hard, crumbly, and bland; next it is sprayed with a culture and left to ripen.

After three weeks minimum, the affinage (cheese maturation) produces the rind,
Its distinctively bloomy, is edible; and has a creamy interior texture well defined.
Another soft cheese made from whole or semi-skimmed cow's-milk is Brie,
Pale in color with grayish tinge, a rind of white mold delicious most will agree.
The curd is drained for about 18 hours after being cast into 20 cm (8 in) molds,
Once thoroughly drained from the molds it is removed and then undergoes.

A process where it is salted and with cheese culture it is inoculated,
Then left to age for at least four or five weeks it is in effect incubated.
If left to mature for several months to a year, the cheese becomes stronger in taste,
The pâte is drier and darker, the rind more crumbly, the flavor is displaced.
An unpleasant amount of ammonia is noticed with overripe Brie,
Baked in a ceramic dish to be served is then best most will agree.

Camembert compared to Brie is softer in texture and has a more pungent aroma,
Has a stronger, slightly sour, chalky taste and when warmed a creamier persona.
Cheddar cheese is off-white, a hard natural cheese or orange to some degree,
If coloured with annatto, an orange-red condiment from the achiote tree.
Sometimes sharp-tasting (i.e., acidic), taking 30 to 40 minutes to set the curd,
Using steel wire knives the curds are cut into half inch cubes preferred.

Gently handling the curds to prevent fat and protein loss to the whey,
They are allowed to set again for 10 to 15 minutes of delay.
For 20–60 minutes the curd is then cooked and is stirred constantly,
Whey is removed from the curds allowing them to drain properly.
Loaves of curds are cut and after ten minutes they are turned over and stacked,
The weight of the loaves on each other helps expel more moisture as they are racked.

When stacks are 4 loaves high, stacking stops but every ten minutes they are turned,
The acidity of the whey is constantly checked until completion is discerned.
The loaves are then cut to a size that fits in a mill that cuts the matted curds,
Into about 1.3 cms (half inch) pieces constantly stirred to avoid re-matting that occurs.
After milling, in salt is thoroughly mixed into molds and in blocks it is pressed,
Mild Cheddar is aged two months, mature for 1 to 12 years is best.

Genevieve liked to tell the story about being on the visitor travel route,

As far as marketing her fromagerie it would be hard to find a substitute.
A bus tour of senior people from Montreal had stopped at the fromagerie,
Who showed a lot of interest in her methods and the cheese she could see.
Genevieve gave them a tour explaining how goat's cheese was made to occur,
She also explained why it was so good and the cheese that they all prefer.

After tasting the cheese she introduced them and had them pet the goats,
Some of the visitors even took notes as she told them several anecdotes.
She showed them a picturesque hillside where many goats were grazing,
They had been put out to pasture, no longer producing, she kept praising.
She then asked, "When your old goats stop producing, what would you do with yours"?
One spry and very quick elderly gentleman answered, "They send us on bus tours."

Cows, and even many goat and sheep to be milked, stand relatively still,
GrandPere couldn't see a good way for rabbits that stillness to fulfill.
And even if there was a way something like a hundred rabbits would be needed,
In order to produce the amount of milk that one cow does before we proceeded.
A rabbit only produces milk for a period of around 6 weeks after giving birth.
So to think of milking rabbits was unthinkable and had absolutely no worth.

This didn't stop GrandPere from inventing outlandish, fantastic miraculous tales,
Of the benefits and cures reaped from drinking rabbit's milk with glorious details.
Cures of all kinds, improved sleep and anxiety and depression relief,
Help to reduce inflammation, treat arthritis and bursitis even though brief.
Rabbits milk was also the domain of many intriguing stories and jokes,
And certainly thought of as being helpful if not wonderful by many folks.

GrandPere teased Genevieve forcing her to rebuke him, she was compelled,
GrandPere laughed at the thought of milking a squirming rabbit being tightly held.
GrandMere encouraged Genevieve to assert herself and firmly stand her ground,

To teach the old fellow that the world has changed and show him what she found.
Genevieve to her credit took out some news articles and some of her notes,
And came out strongly almost imitating her loving strong willed goats.

She noted there are important nutrients for healthy garden soil to make plants grow,
There are three main nutrients, nitrogen-phosphorus-potassium that I know.
Rabbit manure is loaded with all three; having more nitrogen than other animal manure,
Rabbit pellets are higher in phosphorus and potassium also this I am sure.
Rabbit droppings do not have to be composted as other manures do from the start,
Uncomposted they burn plants but not Rabbit manure, also odorless for the most part.

Rabbits are easy to keep, ideal animals for those with limited space,
They are very clean animals and they can be liter box trained just in case.
They are extremely quiet and being very healthy animals they breed,
If you allow them to, they can be raised a whole family to feed.
There's been a lot of research done and we have data on milk yield and composition,
I know that prior to 1969, dealing with rabbit's milk was a mind boggling proposition.

Rabbit milk is rich (12.3 and 12.9 g/100 g) respectively in protein and fat,
2 and 3 times more concentrated in these than cow and sow milk at that.
It has low lactose content (1.7 g/100 g) only one third of the other two,
And high energy content (8.4 MJ/kg) explains how fast the kits grew.
The usual lactation period of does is between 4 and 5 weeks,
But in absence of a new pregnancy, can continue 6 weeks or longer peaks.

Rabbits can be milked by gently pushing the mammary gland,
In one to two minutes one can easily collect 20 ml on demand.
A majority of does have mammary glands and 8 to 10 (nipples) or teats,
Although there is a variation between 6 and 12 with which each competes.
Females with less than 8 teats have a significant lower milk yield,
Than those with 8 or more teats as observed in the field.

Most does take only 3-4 minutes every 24 hours with one nursing event,
For a limited number, nursing their kits more than once a day is spent.
It has not been shown that more milk is produced or that kits grow faster,
When the doe is allowed to perform more than one nursing a day, after.
Exactly the same daily gain, day after day after birth has been observed,
For kits able to suckle their mother freely, only once or twice a day being served.

Finally to prove her point beyond any doubt and beat GrandPere into submission,
Genevieve pulled out a newspaper article and waved it like a true technician.
Over the years I have endured your comical sarcasm and strong opposition,
Of how crazy is the idea of milking rabbits which now requires your recognition.
Scientists in Europe have been doing just that for several years now,
Finding the properties of rabbits milk far better than those of a cow.

NEWS

RABBIT MILK
LEIDEN, THE NETHERLANDS - Dutch farmers are ready to start commercially milking rabbits, pending authorization from European authorities. But that doesn't mean bunny cheese will soon be on store shelves not in Holland anyway. The Dutch genetically engineered rabbits would be milked to churn out a potentially lifesaving drug is developed by Netherlands-based biotech firm Pharming. The rabbits have been outfitted with a human gene that produces a protein called C1 inhibitor. A drug made from the protein is used to treat people with hereditary angioedema (naturally low levels of C1 inhibitor, which can result in episodes of severe swelling, similar to an allergic reaction). Untreated, angioedema can cause painful cramps and potentially fatal suffocation.

Pharming has been milking rabbits experimentally for years, and recently developed a drug called Rhucin from the rabbit milk-derived C1 inhibitor protein. Pharming had submitted Rhucin for market approval by the European Medicines Agency, the European Union body that evaluates drug safety. An official verdict is pending and the drug has yet to be submitted for commercial approval in the United States. Pharming is ready to start milking a herd of about a thousand rabbits once the drug is approved in Europe. The rabbits are milked using mini pumping machines that attach to the female rabbits' teats (nipples). The method can roughly be compared to cow milking, but on a smaller scale of course. Like dairy cows, the rabbits stay relaxed and appear to suffer no discomfort during milking. Researchers then extract the protein in the lab. After extraction the rest of the rabbit milk has to be destroyed due to strict laws governing transgenic products.

Unlike drugs that can be made synthetically in the lab, therapeutic proteins need to be made by biological processes, making transgenic animals a popular option. A rabbit, for instance, can produce an average of 120 milliliters of milk a day. In the modified rabbits, each liter contains 12 grams of human C1 inhibitor. "Human C1 inhibitor can be obtained from donor blood, but the Pharming product can be produced in unlimited quantities from a scalable and stable production system, and there are no safety issues in terms of blood viruses.

The Dutch bunnies wouldn't be the first animals milked in the name of human health. A farm in Russia, for example, recently milked mice to produce the human breast milk protein lactoferrin, and the Russian researchers hope to scale up to milking the protein from goats. But rabbits are particularly well suited to producing certain types of complex proteins that may lead to other new medicines. For instance, transgenic bunnies are also being investigated for potential treatments for stroke victims and organ-transplant patients. Breeding processes are relatively fast (compared to cattle and goats), and milk production is sufficient.

The name "Pharming" comes from a combination of the words farming and pharmaceuticals and is a melding of basic methods of agriculture with advanced biotechnology. Scientists use gene pharming is a technology to alter an animal's own DNA, or to splice in new DNA, called a transgene, from another species. These genetically modified transgenic animals are used mostly to make human proteins that have medicinal value. The protein encoded by the transgene is secreted into the animal's milk, eggs, or blood, and then collected and purified. Livestock such as cattle, sheep, goats, chickens, rabbits, and pigs have already been modified in this way to produce several useful proteins and drugs.

Goats, sheep and rabbits are making their contribution to

> transgenic farming and modern medicine, helping pharmaceutical companies produce drugs to treat diabetes and cancer. Milk from the eastern cottontail rabbit has around 15 percent protein in it—the most protein-rich milk researchers have found so far—and is also rich in fats. According to researchers, milk with high levels of both fats and proteins is seen among species that leave their young unattended for extended periods of time, while the mothers go off to forage. Cottontail rabbit mothers, for instance, return to their ground nests to nurse their young only once or twice a day. During those times when they are nursing, the rabbit pups, called kits, are probably consuming a greater amount of milk, and that milk is going to be higher in density, or richer in nutrients, basically to compensate for the time that they are away from their mothers and are not able to suckle. Following such a rich diet, the young rabbits mature quickly and are able to fend for themselves after only a few weeks of suckling their mother's milk. Milking rabbits has become a reality.

GrandPere rose from his seat and with tears in his eyes went and hugged her so dear,
He apologized for teasing and making her feel bad which he didn't think was so severe.
He was very proud of the fromagerie and the work that she had done,
And he promised never again to tease her even in fun.
GrandPere said that apparently and unintentionally he had made a mistake,
Almost as bad as his friend Félicien, he asked everyone to give him a break.

Félicien arrived home from work in the tannery and for the love of Pete,
Found his dog hanging on to the neighbor's pet rabbit dead in his teeth.
Félicien in a panic knew that Paul, the neighbor would hate him forever, seigneur,
So he took the dirty, chewed-up rabbit, gave it a bath, blow-dried its fur.
Then he put the rabbit back into it's cage hoping that Paul would think it a natural death,
Days later, Paul asked Félicien, "Did you hear that our rabbit took its last breath?"

Félicien stumbled and said, "Um.. no.. what happened?" his surprise not to betray,
Neighbor Paul replied, "We found him peacefully dead in his cage one day,
"Weird thing is, that the day after we buried him we went outside retracing the path,

Someone had dug him up and put him back into the cage after giving him a bath.
There must be some maudite fou (cursed madman) real sick people out there!"
Félicien nobly said, "Unbelievably stupid crazy people all over the place, I swear!"

Genevieve accepted GrandPere's apology and promise no longer to tease,
She in turn said that she was sorry to have complained because it caused her unease.
She appreciated his sense of humour and his views but not the constant reprieve,
She thanked him for his continued advice and support which has helped her to achieve.
It was a very moving moment with demonstrated love on both sides,
All misunderstandings and differences this touching behaviour overrides.

Genevieve pulled out some other news articles that she wanted everyone to know,
Of what was happening in the world, (what's new) quoi de nouveaux.
Many exciting things were happening that we thought were impossible years ago,
Our world knowledge keeps increasing we don't know the changes that we will undergo.
One day an old donkey fell into a well and cried piteously for hours wanting to get out,
The farmers decided it was impossible, the animal was old and not worth it no doubt.

They decided to let him die shovelling dirt to cover up the dry well,
The donkey realizing what was happening cried horribly unable to quell.
Then, to everyone's amazement, he quieted down and let out some happy brays,
A few shovel loads later, they looked down the well their progress to appraise.
Astonished at what they saw. the donkey shook off every shovel of dirt that hit his back,
And took a step up, as they continued to shovel the donkey continued to repack.

He shook it off and took a step up then over the edge of the well he trotted off,

When life shovels dirt on you; the trick is to shake it off and take a step up enough.

The moral is what happens to you isn't nearly as important as how you react to it,

Every adversity may be a stepping stone as long as you never give up and quit.

GrandPere said, "Remember language the donkey could not comprehend or hear,

When others tell you something is impossible sometimes you have to turn a deaf ear.

Genevieve continued to provide some remarkable articles of news, Amazing everyone present with the direction of the research and the reviews.

NEWS

MOOSE CHEESE
STOCKHOLM, SWEDEN - Most cheese is produced from cow, sheep, or goat's milk but it can and is being made from moose milk. Currently, moose milk is sold commercially in both Russia and Sweden. In Russia, moose milk is only supplied for medicinal purposes and is served at upscale sanatoriums and given to kids with gastroenterological diseases. In Sweden, the Elk House (moose are also known as elk in some communities) is the only place in the world that produces the difficult to manufacture cheese from moose milk.

The Elk House (Älgens Hus) farm, a 24-hectare (59-acre) moose dairy farm in Bjursholm, Västerbotten County in northern Sweden, is run by Christer and Ulla Johansson. Bjursholm is about 650 kilometers (404 miles) north of Stockholm. The Johanssons were inspired to set up their farm by the moose milk facilities in eastern Russia but they went one step further and produce moose cheese, the only farm of its kind in Europe. Although there are about 850,000 Moose in Canada, there is no producer of Canadian Moose milk or cheese.

Christer Johannson and his wife Ulla have 14 moose in the fields, but only three "Gullan," "Haelga" and "Juna" can be milked. The three cows, which stay outside all year long, were found as abandoned calves in the woods around Bjursholm and were adopted by the Johannson family. The animals, usually wild, have been domesticated, making it possible to milk them. They weigh about 500 kilograms (1,100 pounds).

Their milk yields roughly 300 kilograms (660 pounds) of cheese per year. The cheese sells for 7,500 kronor (nearly USD 1,000) per kilogram; more precisely about $987 (CAD$) per kilogram or $487 per pound. The moose cheese contains 12% fat, 12% protein, and 21.5% solids such as selenium and zinc. Each animal produces about 5 liters (1.3 gallons) of milk per day. The three cows were abandoned by their mother and adopted by the Johannson family. Moose only lactate from May to September and require the most tender of handling during milking since disturbances can cause the animals to get flustered and dry-up.

The Johanssons personally milk the moose, taking between 30 minutes and two hours to milk a cow, and each produces up to one gallon of milk a day. But that's only between May and September, the time between when they calve and when they are in heat again. Milking is performed in complete silence; if the moose are disturbed they'll dry up. If all goes well, they'll end up with less than two liters per milking session (up to a gallon of milk a day). In comparison, cows give 8 gallons of milk a day. The milk is refrigerated, and curdling is done three times per year, producing about 660 pounds of cheese annually. Moose milking season is very short, and they only get a little bit of milk, for a lot of work during part of the year.

This level of difficulty and the work required naturally translate to a moose-sized cost for this cheese. The moose farm cheese is sold to upscale hotels and restaurants in Sweden. Visitors to the farm can also sample and buy any of the three available cheese varieties; a bloomy rind (like Camembert), a blue cheese, and feta-like cheese. The Elk House attracts about 25,000 visitors a year.

NEWS

REINDEER MILK & CHEESE
HELSINKI, FINLAND - In Scandinavia the tradition of reindeer cheese making is as rich as the reindeer's milk which has long been used. One reindeer yields an average 1.5 cups of milk at each milking session. Even today people make Juustoleipä cheese with reindeer milk. The cheese looks a little like bread, a little like cooked tofu, and a little like the top of a burnt lasagna. It's sometimes called "Finnish Squeaky Cheese" because of the sounds it makes when you bite into a fresh slice of it. Juustoleipä means "cheese bread" in Finnish and the cheese is made in a unique way: Rennet is added to milk

> to form cheese curds. After the curds have been separated they are pressed into a disk shaped pan. The curds are then baked, toasted, or grilled and practically flambéed to create its signature crunchiness and the charred trademark toasty spots on the outside of the loaf. The result is a buttery, fresh cheese with a slightly sweet, caramelized outer crust.
>
> This mild-flavored cheese is very versatile and can be served warm or cold. Most people prefer their bread cheese served warm.. One of the qualities that makes this cheese popular is its grill-ability. It's one of few grillable cheeses that does not melt. When re-heated, this cheese actually stays in one piece but gets creamy and near-melted on the inside, creating a veritable bread-less grilled cheese. Though heat doesn't melt the cheese, it significantly changes its consistency. Cold Juustoleipä is springy and grainy in texture while warm Juustoleipä is silky and smooth with just a little snap to it.

I was most thankful that my experience from earlier today was not mentioned,
But I heard one expression that did make me cringe that later I questioned.
"Tout ça parce qu'il avait la tête pleine de merde", someone had said at the table,
(All because his head was full of shit) it was the merde word I couldn't disable.
"Dans toute chose, il y a un bon côté" *(In all things there is a good side",
GrandPere reminded me that the sensitivity would eventually be pacified.

Wondering, I asked if raw milk straight from the cow was safe to drink?
It might sound natural and good, but raw milk is not safe as you may think.
Raw milk is not pasteurized and poses serious health risks in this era,
Harmful bacteria, such as E. coli O157:H7, Listeria and Salmonella.
Caused serious illnesses such as tuberculosis, diphtheria, and typhoid fever,
Pasteurization killed the harmful bacteria and proved to be a disease reliever.

Pasteurization and homogenization occur at the milk processing plant machine,
After the milk passes through a separator extracting the heavier cream.
The excess milk fat is drawn off and processed into cream or butter,
The milk is fortified with vitamins A and D nutritionally improving the matter.
Pasteurization simply heats milk to 161° Fahrenheit for over 15 seconds,
Then rapidly cooled is extremely effective in preventing infections.

Processed milk also undergoes homogenization with great efficiency,
The fat molecules are broken up producing milk with uniform consistency.
The fat molecules are evenly distributed throughout the milk as a routine,
So that they don't separate and rise to the top forming a layer of cream.
The milk is then quickly cooled to 40° F (4.4° C) to avoid harming its taste,
Then it is packaged into glass bottles, coated paper cartons or plastic bags in haste.

I learned some history, how in 1970 a supply management system was put in place,
By government of Canada to reduce the surplus in production that had been embraced.
In the 1950s - 1960s, and to ensure a fair return on farmers production costs,
So in 1970, the National Milk Marketing Plan came into effect to control supply stocks.
The national supply system for eggs in 1972, turkey in 1974, was implemented,
And for chicken in 1978 and chicken hatching eggs in 1986, it was extended.

Each supply managed farm owns quota (market share) for an amount of production,
Based on demand, the amount can be increased / decreased is the assumption.
Overproduction is avoided because production is kept in sync with demand,
Enabling farmers to directly earn a predictable and stable revenue as planned.
The Federal and Provincial governments both share in making the system function,
Quota adjustments are made on an as-required basis; either increases or reduction.

A quota is defined as 1 kg butterfat per day (production of one dairy cow) as a marquee,
Quotas are akin to guaranties of a market share and at first these quotas were free,
But to have more and more quotas was the only way increased revenues could be.

Producers traded quotas among themselves; creating a competition for quotas greedily,
So they quickly took on value very dramatically and increased appreciably.
Left to itself, without ethical safeguards, a race for quotas occurred in each commodity.

The sale of quotas is recorded from $17,282 in 1998 increasing to $30,840 in 2006,
Finally being capped at $25,000 in 2010 and that capped value still persists.
The province requires a minimum quota of 10 kg in order to start production,
$250,000 is needed to buy quotas in order to milk 10 cows; that is an obstruction,
For any new farmer before buying a single cow, a farm, equipment for production;
That's supposing quotas are even available, which they rarely are, bad presumption.

The Minister of Agriculture is responsible for the (CDC) Canadian Dairy Commission.
Determining the price that farmers receive for raw milk is the Commission's mission.
The CDC (Commission canadienne du lait) also chairs the Canadian Milk Supply
Management Committee, coordinating milk production and ensure they comply.
The CDC with provincial officials are mandated to obtain farmers a fair return,
When setting milk price, production costs and consumers' ability to pay are of concern.

Milk demand is predicted by the Canadian Dairy Commission (CDC) for the,
Canadian Milk Supply Management Committee (CMSMC) for quota comme ca.
The CMSMC allocates milk production among the provinces to each board,
Which in turn allocates its share of milk production among quota holders on record.
The boards buy all the milk produced in the province at a guaranteed price;
Milk revenues are then pooled and paid back to producers to be precise.

In 1983 was formed the Fédération des producteurs de lait du Québec (FPLQ),
In 2014, the FPLQ became Les Producteurs de lait du Québec (PLQ).
PLQ has the responsibility of negotiating on their behalf all sales terms and crisis,
They negotiate and work together through milk quality rules and raw material prices.
The règlements are set and Genevieve, an artisan cheese maker in her own barn,
Has to pay milk transport fees to the PLQ even though the milk is from their own farm.

Dairy farmers were almost solely dependent on milk revenues and felt a threat,
Selling a highly perishable product they had to adopt a market-oriented mindset.
They were at a market disadvantage since they depended on a few regional buyers,
To counteract these buyers, farmers created dairy cooperatives with new aspires.
The 1990s, saw Saputo, Parmalat and Agropur became multinational and factual,
Quebec cooperative Agropur, operates in Canada, U.S.A. and South America actual.

Interesting to note that domestic consumption is set on the federal level with no friction,
While what can be produced outside of a quota is under provincial jurisdiction.
Production outside of a quota are products for personal use and direct sale,
But there are rules that even production outside of a quota are curtailed.
In Quebec, milk cows non quota are not allowed while turkeys are limited to 25,
100 is the limit for each of chickens and egg laying hens that are alive.

Outside quota production requires farmers to pay an annual $20 permit fee,
But also most importantly they must record and present their data regularly.
High tariffs on imports ensure that domestic prices are not undercut or squeezed,
Tariffs are 238% for whole chickens, 299% for butter, 246% for cheese,

155% for whole turkeys, 164% for shell eggs and for these,
And also not to forget 238% for hatching eggs if you please.

Before milking machines, milking by hand was quite a determined chore,
Perseverance, technique and a lot of hard work; patience it did underscore.
Etienne the old timer remembered those former times very well,
Happy to see those times long gone his story is easy now for him to tell.
He was sitting in the Auberge bar having whisky blanc, getting drunk,
Asked why?, Etienne replied, "Some things you just can't explain, it stunk."

"So what happened that's so bad?" Bastien, the owner, asked sitting down next to him,
Etienne said, "The cow kicked over the full bucket with her left leg.", rubbing his chin.
Scratching his head Bastien said, "That's not so bad",
Etienne replied, "Some things you just can't explain, very sad."
Filling Etienne's glass, "So what happened then?" Bastien enquired.
Etienne gulped his whiskey, seemed baffled but continued not being tired.

"I took her left leg and tied it to the post on the left." Etienne replied,
"Then with another bucket filled, she kicked it over with her right leg in one stride".
"Some things you just can't explain as an oversight."
"I took her right leg this time and tied it to the post on the right."
Shaking his head in sympathy Bastien asked, ""So, what did you do then?"
Etienne replied, "Well, I sat back down and began milking her again.

"Just as I got the bucket full, the stupid cow knocked over the bucket with her tail."
"Hmmm," Bastien said nodding his head. "So, what did you do, give me some detail?"
"Well, I ran out of rope, I tied her tail to the rafter with my suspenders, having no belt,"
"In that moment, my pants fell down; my wife and the Curée walked in, ashamed I felt.
"Some things you just can't explain, no matter how hard you try."
"Why they came in just then? and why the Curée too, Why?"

GrandPere was fortunate to have such a supportive family who got along together,
There were many families where goodwill and harmony did not prevail however.

GrandPere told me a story about his old friend Rene originally from Trois Pistoles,
Whose son Jean Louis in his youth was always short of money and on the dole.
Situated in the Bas-Saint-Laurent region with Île aux Basques island just offshore,
Although having lost his money Rene continues his only son to adore.

Jean Louis was accepted to attend the Universitè de Montreal,
With $1,000 dollars and Rene's blessing he was sent off in the fall.
After one month Rene got a letter asking for another $1,000 with some stress,
Signing the letter as "Your ever-loving son, Jean Louis, BS."
Weighing the request with considerable thought, Rene dug up the dough,
Buried in his garden secret spot, he sent it, hoping it would last awhile you know.

Imagine his surprise when in a month he received another urgent request,
This time the letter was signed, "Your ever-loving son, Jean Louis, BS., MS."
Old Rene was puzzled by the initials after his son's name he could not ignore,
Both the Curée and notaire thought they were academic accreditations for sure.
Rene again dug up the money and sent it, hoping it would bring success,
But remarking how expensive education was, he was somewhat depress.

He heard nothing at Noel from his loving son, nothing for another month and days,
Finally a letter apologizing for missing Noel, a very busy time for his son it conveys.
This time the letter is signed, "Your ever-loving son, Jean Louis, BS., MS., PhD,"
The Curée and notaire after seeing this say that Jean Louis is a doctor they all agree.
Rene is proud as can be, but found the request for $5,000 caused him much stress,
He could not back out now when it was needed the most so he sent it nevertheless.

Again he heard nothing for three months and more days spent waiting hoping to hear,
Checking his mailbox, when to his surprise, unannounced, who should appear.
Jean Louis was home at last, Rene welcomed him making his heart soar,
After lunch he congratulated his son on the initials after his name he could not ignore.
Referring to the last letter Rene asked his son, Jean Louis for some clarification,
Rene said, "The Curée and notaire said you were a Docteur with no reservation.

Jean Louis apologized profusely to Rene for all the confusion that resulted,
He slowly explained the meaning and he hoped that everyone would not be insulted.
He was making a joke saying BS stood for bullshit that I overcame,
While MS said that there was more, meaning more of the same.
Jean Louis said PhD stood for piled higher and deeper not a doctor degree,
Stunned, to be made a fool of is something that old Rene did not foresee.

Anyway old Rene stood by his son but never gave him more money that we could see,
Old Rene moved here, his son got married lives in Montreal with wife Natalie.
Rene gets a letter from them, his vision is not very well, but he is aware,
So GrandPere keeps in touch, gets to read his mail to him and takes him everywhere.
After the last letter GrandPere exclaimed, "C'est dur pour lui, car il es pleine de merde".
(It's probably just hard for him because he is so full of shit), a laugh they shared.

Jean Louis's letter described his emergency room visit with bruises and bleeding head,
When the doctor asked him what happened. "Well, it was like this" Jean Louis said.
"I was having a wonderfully quiet round of golf with my wife, when dead ahead,
Was the most difficult hole in the entire course, we both sliced our balls instead.
Both sailed into a lush green pasture of cows with no sound,
We went to look for them, and while I was rooting around,

I noticed that one of the cows had something white in it's rear end.
I walked over and lifted up the tail, and sure enough, hard to comprehend,
A golf ball with my wife's monogram on it stuck right in the middle of the cow's butt,
I was delighted but that is when I should have kept my mouth shut.
"What did you do?", asked the doctor. I said, "That's when I made my mistake."
"Well, I pointed, and yelled to my wife, "Hey! This looks like yours for God's sake!"

"Her yelling and screams I still hear reverberating in my head,
I am seeing double, head is throbbing, maybe soon I will be dead."
The doctor said, "You have a bad concussion probably from the golf club crash,"
You will need some rest I recommend that you stay in bed to heal the large gash.
You may experience headaches, dizziness, fatigue, sleep problems, and irritability,
These will go away on their own within months but watch for susceptibility.

Rene fondly remembered Jean Louis's response to a question in school,
La maîtresse a demandé – Quel est le futur de "je bâille" ? without ridicule,
(The teacher asked – What is the future tense of 'I yawn'?
Without giving much thought or even hesitating thereon,
Jean Louis with a big smile answered – Je dors ! (I sleep!).
Another answer that Rene said in his memory he would always keep,

Was when the teacher asked him if his father helped him with his homework?
To which Jean Louis replied – NON! M'dame, je vous jure! with a smirk.
(No! Miss, I swear he didn't!) Are you sure? Oui, Il l'a fait tout seul, bien sur.
(Yes, He did it all by himself, for sure); called in to school I had to concur.
Rene felt bad that his son was badly hurt and may affect him later on,
Fearing Rene would get sick, GrandPere encouraged him not to dwell thereupon

GrandMere motioned to me and taking me to one side,
Handed me a laundry bag all very neatly tied.

All of my clothes had been washed, ironed and neatly pressed,
She said, "I should take it with me for demain (tomorrow) to get dressed.
Demain I could give Camille's clothes that I was not using,
To GrandPere who would pick me up for a trip we'd be sharing.

Clutching the laundry bag, I thanked her sincerely, kissing both cheeks,
Hadn't had that kind of wonderful service for many weeks.
Washing and ironing for me was a weekly unwelcoming chore,
And here it was tied with a bow. done really well long before.
She cautioned that the long sous vêtements I should wear,
(Long underwear) For the duration while I was there.

GrandPere recalled when two ladies checked in at the Auberge their reservation,
He was there and listened as Bastien gave them details and information.
Bastien had said, "The bar is open 24 hours for auberge guests and delights."
Shocked one of the women said. "Only 24 hours? But we are here four nights."
Bastien looks at her dumbfounded, speechless and scratches his head,
The other woman said "Don't worry about her, we had a long trip and going to bed",

Getting ready to return to the Auberge, GrandPere asked me how long I was to stay,
I planned to stay for two weeks; he urged me to reconsider since I came from faraway.
He suggested after my two weeks at the Auberge I consider a free no charge getaway,
To stay with his wife and him, his family for a real snowy experience and breakaway.
That became the basis of my plan getting the opportunity to enjoy the festive holiday,
As well as the camaraderie, customs and delicious delicacies that I could never repay.

The wind she blow and billow wafts of swirling chimney smoke,
She whistle and blow so hard I think the trees she will broke.
The blinding snow make it hard to look up and see the sky.
The wind she carry the snow piling it in drifts everywhere very high,
If you are asked to "donner un coup de main," don't punch that person dear,

They ask for "give a helping hand", smile and say (yes, with pleasure) "oui, avec plaisir".

There was always that little part of me that knew saying goodbye was coming sooner than later. Then rather suddenly it could not be put off any longer. I could never prepare myself fully to say goodbye. It was too painful to consider. Tomorrow was my planned departure and GrandPere was to take me in his sleigh to the train station. We had a party the day before I had to leave at the centre d'acceuil. Almost everyone was there and many words were exchanged. Even the Curee blessed me and prayed for my safe journey home. That evening the cold wind blew as hard as ever. As GrandPere would say, " She blow so hard, she ring the church bell." But at least it was not snowing. I was presented with a beautiful woolen scarf and a pair of long underwear to remind me to return some day. There was no way of saying a quick goodbye as if you will see them tomorrow. What made it so hard was that we all knew that we would not be seeing one another again. They wanted me to know that no matter how long we went without seeing each other that they will always be there for me. Their goodbyes was just another way of saying 'I love you'.

I have no idea how, or even if, my time with GrandPere and all these wonderful people will impact me in the future, but it doesn't matter. I set out wanting to see snow and how people got used to it. What I found was precious loving memories of people who I probably will never see again. They were part of and touched my life. Living with every single person in that village is part of my history. I value those friendships more than anything else, and it will be those relationships that I will remember from my Quebec adventure forever. It seems that everything in life happens for a reason and we don't always know why. With tears streaming down our face we trust God to lead the way and say Goodbye. Saying Goodbye really hurt knowing that I may never return but we had no other choice but to move on. We wave at each other as the train pulls away. Au Revoir GrandPere Anctil and GrandMere Marie Rose et toute la famille. What a sad Goodbye that had to happen, no matter how much it hurt.

FIN   END

ABOUT THE AUTHOR

As a business consultant, Roman travelled extensively throughout Canada, the U.S. and the Caribbean, speaking at various engagements, meeting many people in diverse walks of life and exchanging life experiences with them. He authored several articles and courses in finance and was awarded several academic awards. He was the professor at George Brown College in Toronto that students called "the best teacher", noting his charisma, enthusiasm and sense of humour.
Find out more about Roman at romansemporium.com.

Made in the USA
Columbia, SC
04 April 2021